WOODTURNER'S PROJECT BOOK

Phil Jones &
Charles Mercer

Sterling Publishing Co., Inc.   New York

Edited by Laurel Ornitz

Library of Congress Cataloging-in-Publication Data

Jones, Phil.
   Woodturner's project book.

   Includes index.
   1. Turning.   I. Mercer, Charles.   II. Title.
TT201.J66   1987   684'.083   86-23077
ISBN 0-8069-6478-2 (pbk.)

Copyright © 1987 by Phillip Jones & Charles Mercer
Published by Sterling Publishing Co., Inc.
Two Park Avenue, New York, N.Y. 10016
Distributed in Canada by Oak Tree Press Ltd.
℅ Canadian Manda Group, P.O. Box 920, Station U
Toronto, Ontario, Canada M8Z 5P9
Distributed in the United Kingdom by Blandford Press
Link House, West Street, Poole, Dorset BH15 1LL, England
Distributed in Australia by Capricorn Ltd.
P.O. Box 665, Lane Cove, NSW 2066
Manufactured in the United States of America
All rights reserved

CONTENTS

INTRODUCTION

The projects in this book are intended for woodturners who wish to extend their range of ideas and techniques to produce an array of wood-turned objects for everyday use.

The necessary tools and lathe accessories, as well as suggested types of wood, appear at the beginning of each set of instructions. The turning methods that follow have been selected because of their traditional application and proven efficiency. However, new equipment and accessories are also included for the production of several items to demonstrate their advantages over older methods.

The projects are arranged in an increasing order of complexity. On a scale of A to C, A should be well within the capabilities of the novice who has mastered the use of the basic six tools—roughing gouge, skew chisel, straight-across chisel, spindle gouge, beading and parting tool, and fluted parting tool.

The most difficult pieces are the Magician's Eggcup and the Traveller's Cup because they require extremely accurate turning to produce the closely fitting components. If the instructions and illustrations are followed carefully, both these projects will show the excellence and skill that can be attained in wood turning.

Since the design and decoration of the projects in this book are not intended to be definitive, there's ample room for modification if desired. All the tool work is done according to the cutting method (rather than the scraping method), unless the use of a scraping tool is specifically required.

When a piece, such as a vase or a pepper pot, has a large hole drilled through the middle, it's necessary to use plugs. Instructions on making plugs are found in Chapter 44.

Although finishing methods are left to the turner's individual preference, different methods are suggested for the various projects. These methods are explained in Chapter 45.

Happy turning!

1
TOOL HANDLE

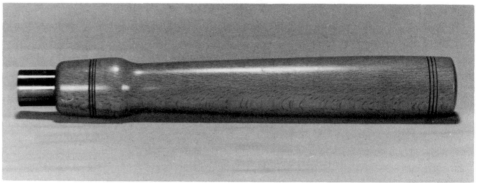

Illus. 1.

WOOD

Beech or ash or any straight-grained hardwood
2″ × 2″ × 12″
Tubing for ferrule to suit tang of tool

LATHE ACCESSORIES

Four-pronged driving center
Dead center and revolving center
Jacob's chuck
Drill bit, ⅜″ for tang
Long tool rest

OTHER TOOLS

Roughing gouge
Skew chisel, 1¼″
Spindle gouge
Beading and parting tool

FINISHING

Method 1

DIFFICULTY

Grade A

1. Find the middle of the blank and then drive in the four-pronged driving center in order to leave a mark at both ends. This will make realignment easier when you reverse the work. Place the Jacob's chuck in the headstock and, holding the blank against the dead center for support, drill a hole with the ⅜″ bit to a depth of 2½″ for the tang (Illus. 2).

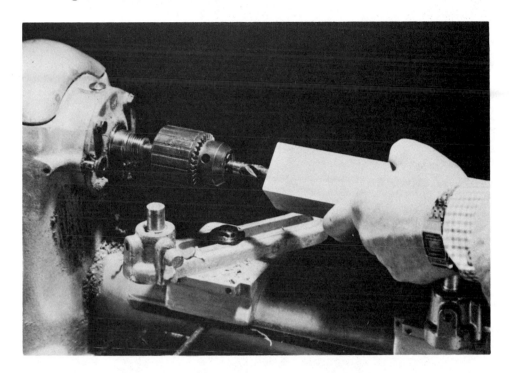

Illus. 2. Drill hole for tang.

2. Set the four-pronged center into the marks previously made; then place the ferrule over the dead center and push the dead center into the hole, fixing the assembly between centers on the lathe (Illus. 3). Rough down to the largest diameter, square the end grain with the skew, and then scribe a mark on the end of the cylinder a little shorter than the length of the ferrule.

Turn a spigot for the ferrule, stopping the lathe frequently to check the ferrule for a tight fit. To help in establishing the correct diameter, use a taper to the right-hand end of the spigot. Take care when fitting the ferrule to the spigot because it can jam when it's only halfway in position.

3. Before finally fitting the ferrule, undercut the shoulder with the skew to hide the ferrule end. When you are satisfied with the fit (Illus. 4), use a hammer and block to force on the ferrule and replace the dead center with a revolving center.

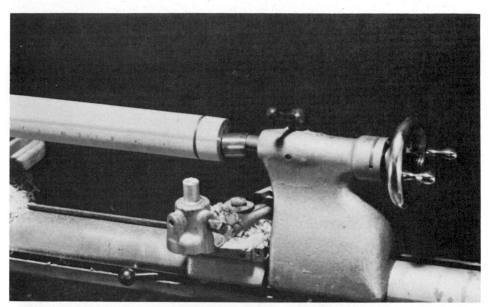

Illus. 3. Ferrule rests on dead center.

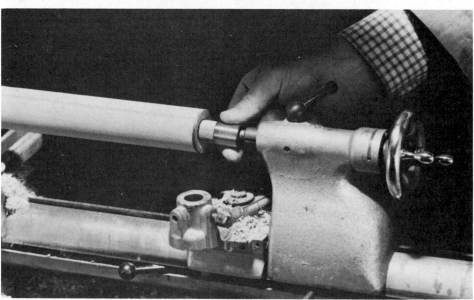

Illus. 4. Ferrule and dead center in position.

4. Rough out the handle design (Illus. 5) and cut gripping grooves at both ends of the handle (Illus. 6). Buff the ferrule with steel wool, but finish the handle with abrasives only.

5. Remove the handle and note the marks left by the four-pronged center at the ferrule end. Reverse it, using the marks to relocate the driving center. The piece may not be exactly dead center when you reverse it; but you can cut the shoulder with the skew without any trouble, leaving a small holding pip over the revolving center (Illus. 6). Finish completely, according to Method 1 on page 213 or to your own preference.

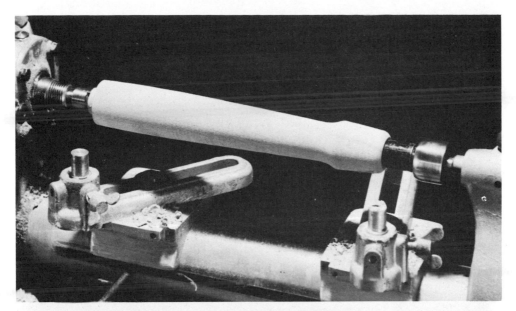

Illus. 5. Rough out handle design.

Illus. 6. The finished shoulder.

2
KNIFE HANDLE

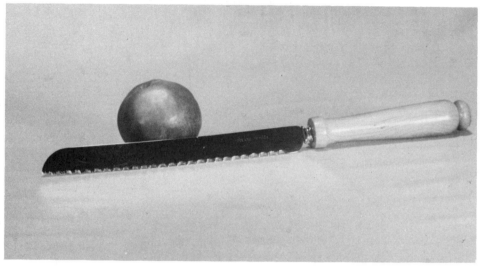

Illus. 7.

WOOD

Any hardwood to suit knife
   blade
1¼″ × 1¼″ × 6″

LATHE ACCESSORIES

Four-pronged driving center
Revolving center
Jacob's chuck
Drill bit to suit blade tang

OTHER TOOLS

Roughing gouge
Skew chisel, 1¼″
Spindle gouge
Beading and parting tool

FINISHING

Method 1 or 4

DIFFICULTY

Grade A

1. Drill a hole for the tang of the knife blade, following the method described for the tool handle in Chapter 1. Place the drilled blank between the centers, with the revolving center in the hole, and rough down to the basic design (Illus. 8).

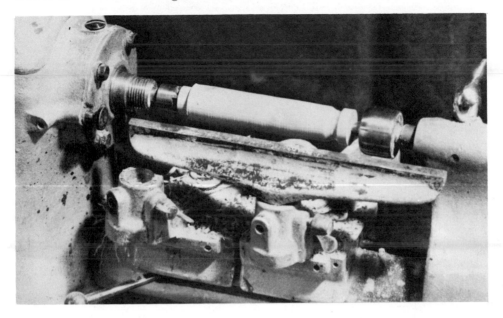

Illus. 8. The roughed-out blank.

2. To save time in production, you can use the roughing gouge to shape the handle (Illus. 9). Use the beading and parting tool to form any beads in the design, and then finish according to Method 1 on page 213, Method 4 on page 214, or to your own preference.

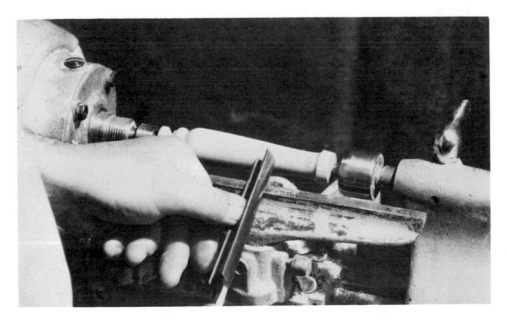

Illus. 9. Shaping with the gouge.

3. Be sure to buff the wax to a high shine. Note the holding pip at the headstock end of the work, which is parted with the skew so that you can obtain a neat finish (Illus. 10).

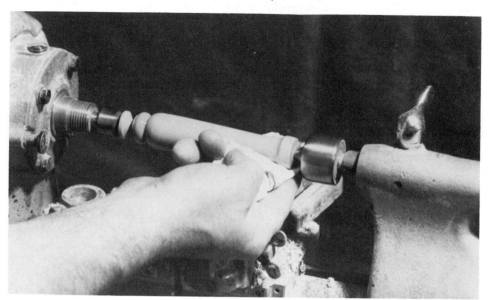

Illus. 10. Note holding pip at headstock.

3
SPINNING TOP

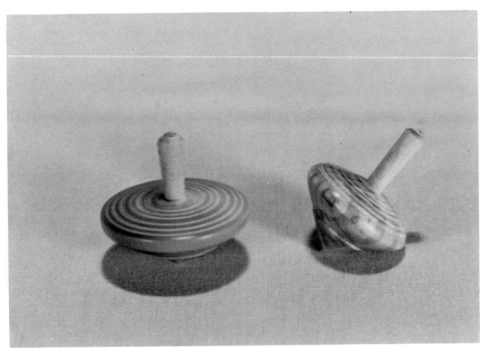

Illus. 11.

WOOD	Any remnants—an ideal project for small waste pieces
LATHE ACCESSORIES	Screw chuck Revolving center
OTHER TOOLS	Roughing gouge Skew chisel, 1¼″ Spindle gouge
FINISHING	Method 3
DIFFICULTY	Grade A

1. Fix the blank on the screw chuck and, using the revolving center to keep it steady, rough down to the largest diameter. Make a cone shape at the end of the cylinder with a small spindle gouge (Illus. 12). Remove the revolving center.

Illus. 12. Cone at end of cylinder.

2. First shape the top and then remove the waste to form the stem (Illus. 13).

Illus. 13. Shape top and stem.

3. While the stem is still thick, glass-paper the top body completely and then reduce the stem, creating a fine taper from left to right (Illus. 14). Part off and then finish with a durable polyurethane varnish (see Method 3 on page 214) or paint in bright gloss colors.

This project is a great favorite with children of all ages.

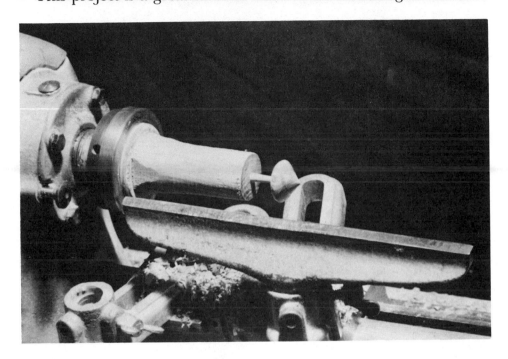

Illus. 14. Ready for parting.

4
DRAWER KNOB

Illus. 15.

WOOD	Use any suitable size. If required as a replacement, a suitable grain and color match are also essential. Ideal for remnants.
LATHE ACCESSORIES	Screw chuck Revolving center
OTHER TOOLS	Roughing gouge Skew chisel, 1¼″ Beading and parting tool Spindle gouge, ¼″
FINISHING	Use any finish that suits the drawer front.
DIFFICULTY	Grade A

1. Determine the size of the finished knob and, having selected a suitable piece of wood, rough down to the largest diameter (Illus. 16). Dome the end of the cylinder with the skew to form the top of the knob.

Illus. 16. The prepared blank.

2. Mark the cylinder with the dimensions of the knob, making sure that the lines fall where the gouge will change its direction of action. To avoid interference with the flowing line of the knob head, cut the basal ring first. This allows the gouge easier access in forming the cove behind the head of the knob (Illus. 17). The shoulder of the base also acts as a fence for the gouge.

Illus. 17. Note shallow cove to prevent wobble of knob head.

3. Before making the cove too deep, work on the end grain of the head to produce a flowing curve. Determine the thickness of the basal ring, scribe, and then reduce with the beading and parting tool. Slightly undercut the base to ensure a flush fit against the drawer surface and turn a spigot to a known drill size, tapering the cut towards the left-hand end to permit easy insertion into the drawer front (Illus. 18).

Illus. 18. The finished design, showing taper on spigot.

5
LIGHT PULL

Illus. 19.

WOOD Use mahogany, elm, cherry, yew, or any hardwood with an attractive grain. Old chair legs are ideal.
1″ × 1″ × 2½″

LATHE ACCESSORIES Four-pronged driving center
Revolving center
Jacob's chuck
Plug to cover driving center
Long series drill bits, ⅛″ and ¼″

OTHER TOOLS Roughing gouge
Beading and parting tool
Spindle gouge

FINISHING Method 3

DIFFICULTY Grade A

1. Place the Jacob's chuck in the lathe and, using the ⅛″ bit, drill the first hole to accommodate the string (Illus. 20). Keep the lathe speed on a low setting because it's important to keep this hole as central as possible. Take care not to drill into the revolving center. Reverse the workpiece and drill the ¼″ hole to a depth of ½″. This hole will later hide the knotted string. (See Illus. 21.)

Illus. 20. Drilling the first hole.

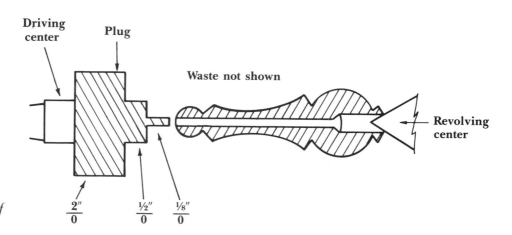

Illus. 21. Cross section of light pull.

2. Illus. 21 shows the completed profile of the light pull, with the central hole and the larger hole in the base. Note the spigot on the

plug, which is turned down to ⅛″. You must use care when roughing down because this point is very fragile.

3. Insert a suitable plug (see Chapter 44) and rough down carefully to the largest diameter (Illus. 22).

Illus. 22. The cylinder ready for the gouge.

4. You can use the roughing gouge to save time or form the basic shape with a spindle gouge (Illus. 23).

Illus. 23. The basic shape

5. With the beading and parting tool, score the outside of the cylinder in preparation for rolling the bead shapes with the beading and parting tool. Note the pip remaining over the revolving center, which may be left as part of the design (Illus. 24). Use a glass paper finish and, for extra protection since the pull is handled frequently, a durable finish, such as polyurethane varnish (see Method 3 on page 214).

Illus. 24. The completed light pull.

6
CANDLE LAMP

Illus. 25.

WOOD	Any wood that suits the lamp glass 3½″ × 3½″ × 6″
OTHER MATERIALS	Lamp glass
LATHE ACCESSORIES	Spigot chuck Revolving center Jacob's chuck Drill bit to suit candle
OTHER TOOLS	Roughing gouge Skew chisel, 1¼″

Spindle gouge
Beading and parting tool
Fluted parting tool

FINISHING

Method 1

DIFFICULTY

Grade A

1. Prepare the wood between centers for the spigot chuck, insert, and then rough down to the largest diameter. Square the end grain with the skew, and drill a hole ½″ deep to suit the base of the candle (Illus. 26).

Illus. 26. Drill hole for candle.

2. Measure the internal diameter of the base of the lamp glass and subtract ⅒″. Transfer this measurement to the end of the cylinder. Scribe the cylinder ½″ from the end and form a rabbet down to your mark (Illus. 27). (The ½″ rabbet will ensure that the glass will not fall over if the lamp is knocked down while in use.) Undercut the shoulder with the skew to provide a firm seat for the lamp glass.

Illus. 27. Form the rabbet.

3. Scribe a line to delineate the base, stem, and bowl (Illus. 28). Finish to your own design or according to Method 1 on page 213. Apply polish and part off, undercutting the base to make sure it will stand squarely.

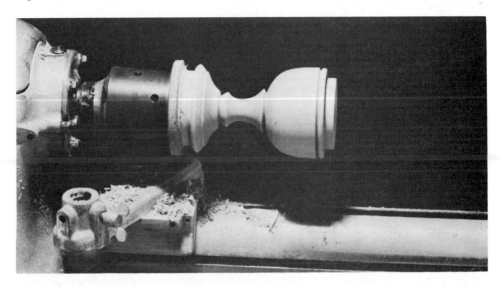

Illus. 28. Note clean lines of base, stem, and bowl.

4. Fit the candle and lamp glass. You don't need to drill holes into the lamp base for carbon dioxide to escape because the lamp glass shown in Illus. 29 provides enough updraft to keep the air moving and the candle burning.

Illus. 29. Assemble the components.

7
DRIED-FLOWER VASE

Illus. 30.

WOOD

Anything suitable
3″ × 3″ × 4″

LATHE ACCESSORIES

Spigot chuck
Large saw-toothed machine
center bit

OTHER TOOLS	Roughing gouge
	Skew chisel, 1¼″
	Beading and parting tool
	Spindle gouge
	Straight-across scraper
FINISHING	Method 1
DIFFICULTY	Grade A

1. Fix the workpiece into the spigot chuck and rough down to the largest diameter. Drill out the middle and widen with the scraper to the required diameter (Illus. 31). No further finish is required inside because you will fill the cavity with Plasticine for the dried-flower stems.

Illus. 31. Remove waste.

2. Transfer the inside depth onto the outside of the cylinder and scribe a line. Delineate the base and scribe another line. Working towards the base, cut a cove with the spindle gouge and form the base to your own design (Illus. 32). For a professional finish, form a lip around the opening and accentuate it by placing a fine line just below it with the beading and parting tool (Illus. 33).

Illus. 32. Work cove towards base.

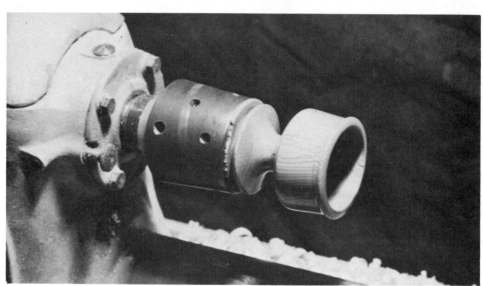

Illus. 33. Note line below lip.

3. Glass-paper and finish according to Method 1 on page 213 or to your own preference.

8
BUD VASE

Illus. 34.

WOOD   Anything suitable, including
                        small offcuts

OTHER MATERIALS   Glass vial to fit inside vase

LATHE ACCESSORIES   Four-pronged driving center
                        Revolving center
                        Jacob's chuck and suitable drill
                        bit
                        Plug

OTHER TOOLS   Roughing gouge
                        Skew chisel, 1¼″

Spindle gouge
Beading and parting tool
Fluted parting tool

FINISHING   Method 1 or 4

DIFFICULTY   Grade A

1. Find the centers of the blank, and then drill a hole in one end slightly larger than the diameter of the glass vial (to allow for expansion) and to the required depth. Insert the plug at the tailstock end (Illus. 35). For instructions on making your own plug, turn to Chapter 44.

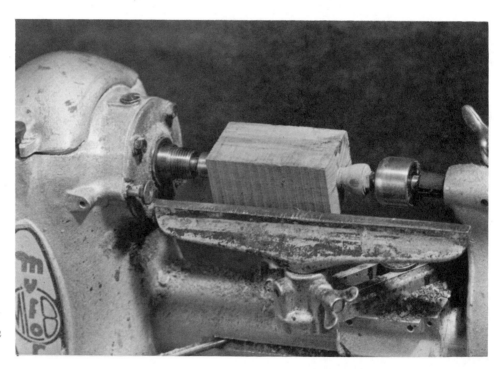

Illus. 35. The blank with plug insert.

2. Rough down to a cylinder, delineate the base, and rough out the basic design (Illus. 36). Use a spindle gouge to shape the bulbous base, keeping the lines flowing.

3. Finish with abrasives and part off (Illus. 37). If you will be filling the vial with water, it's advisable to apply plastic coat finish to the vase (see Method 4 on page 214). If you will be using the vase for dried flowers, you should use Method 1 on page 213.

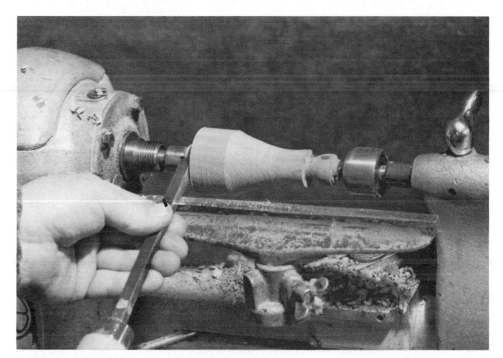

Illus. 36. Rough out basic design.

Illus. 37. Finished base ready for parting.

4. As an alternative to a solid blank, you can select two pieces of wood with interesting grain figures, glue them together with a sandwich of veneer in between, and leave them overnight to dry (Illus. 38).

*Illus. 38. The split
blank.*

5. Turn as described for the solid piece (Illus. 39).

Illus. 39. Finished vase.

Illus. 1. Inlaid vanity mirror.

Illus. 2. Pomander.

Illus. 3. Apples and pears.

A

Illus. 4. From left to right: light pull, lace bobbin, spinning tops, traditional needlecase, drawer knob, cigar holder, and ring tree.

Illus. 5. From left to right: needlecase, pepper pot, coin saver, antique beehive box, and box with integral lid.

B

Illus. 6. Candle lamp.

Illus. 7. Magician's eggcup.

Illus. 8. Boxes—inlaid and plain.

C

Illus. 9. Eggcup.

Illus. 10. Log table lamp.

Illus. 11. From left to right: goblets with lids, eggcup, candlestick, napkin ring, pepper grinder, and salt grinder.

D

tool

for the chuck
, fix the work-
meter using the

ONAL
ASE

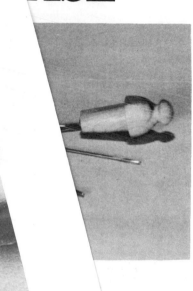

ined

drill to a depth of 2½"

sert

the outside of the case,
hand side since this area

t with

according to Method 1 on
then part off.
for a snug fit (Illus. 44).

FINISHING

Method 1

DIFFICULTY

Grade A

1. Fix the blank between centers and turn the spigo
insert. With the insert in position in the spigot chuc
piece between centers and reduce to the largest dia
roughing gouge (Illus. 41).

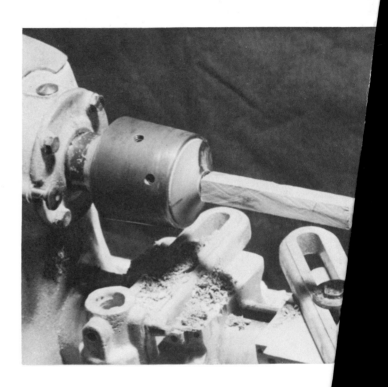

*Illus. 41. Blank and
insert in chuck.*

2. Square the end with the skew chisel and
(Illus. 42).

3. Replace the revolving center and shape
working carefully at the waste on the left-
will be used for the plug (Illus. 43). Finish
page 213 or to your own preference, and

4. Make the plug, creating a long taper
Finish and part off.

9
TRADITIONAL NEEDLECASE

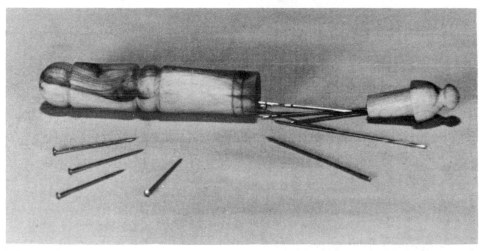

Illus. 40.

WOOD

Any attractively grained
   hardwood
¾" × ¾" × 5"

LATHE ACCESSORIES

Spigot chuck with insert
Revolving center
Jacob's chuck, or drill bit with
   morse taper shank
Drill bit, ⁵⁄₁₆"
Miniature four-pronged
   driving center

OTHER TOOLS

Roughing gouge
Skew chisel, 1¼"

Spindle gouge
Beading and parting tool

FINISHING　　　　　Method 1

DIFFICULTY　　　　　Grade A

1. Fix the blank between centers and turn the spigot for the chuck insert. With the insert in position in the spigot chuck, fix the workpiece between centers and reduce to the largest diameter using the roughing gouge (Illus. 41).

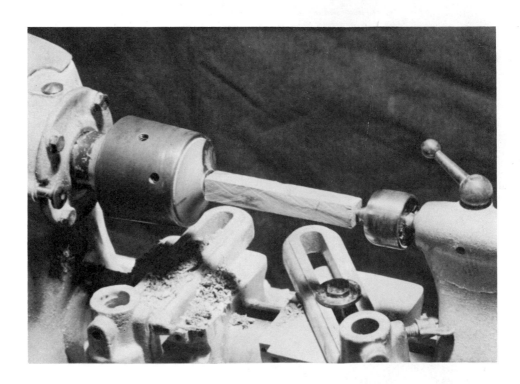

Illus. 41. Blank and insert in chuck.

2. Square the end with the skew chisel and drill to a depth of 2½″ (Illus. 42).

3. Replace the revolving center and shape the outside of the case, working carefully at the waste on the left-hand side since this area will be used for the plug (Illus. 43). Finish according to Method 1 on page 213 or to your own preference, and then part off.

4. Make the plug, creating a long taper for a snug fit (Illus. 44). Finish and part off.

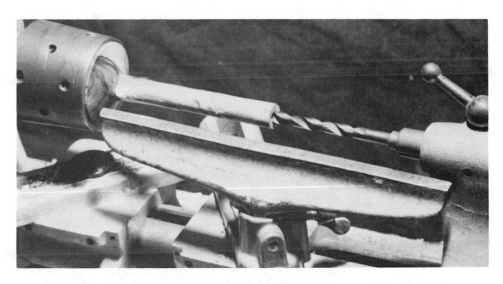

Illus. 42. Drill out waste.

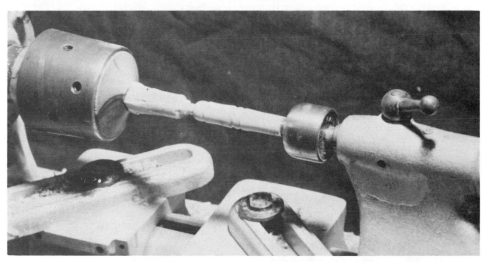

Illus. 43. Shape the outside.

Illus. 44. The completed plug.

10
POTATO MASHER/ FRUIT PULPER

Illus. 45.

WOOD

Sycamore or beech or any
wood that is nontoxic
Head: 3″ × 3″ × 5″
Handle: 1¼″ × 1¼″ × 14″

LATHE ACCESSORIES

Four-pronged driving center
Revolving center
Jacob's chuck
Drill bit, ⅝″
Plug

OTHER TOOLS

Roughing gouge
Skew chisel, 1¼″

Spindle gouge
Beading and parting tool
Straight-across chisel, 1¼"

FINISHING Fine abrasive paper only

DIFFICULTY Grade A

1. You need to make the masher block first (Illus. 46). Place the blank between centers and rough down to the largest diameter. Square the end with the skew.

Illus. 46. Cylinder for masher head.

2. Replace the revolving center with a Jacob's chuck and the ⅝" drill bit, and drill a hole 1" deep (Illus. 47).

Illus. 47. Drill hole.

3. Replace the revolving center, fit a plug into the masher head (Illus. 48), and fix between centers. True the cylinder with the gouge again if necessary, and square the end with the skew.

Illus. 48. Fit plug.

4. Delineate the base and score with a line; then reduce with the beading and parting tool to a spigot at the headstock end. You must keep the form simple so that you can clean the utensil easily. With the straight-across chisel, plane the cylinder first with a slight taper from left to right (Illus. 49). Note the height of the tool rest and the chisel working on the top of the cylinder.

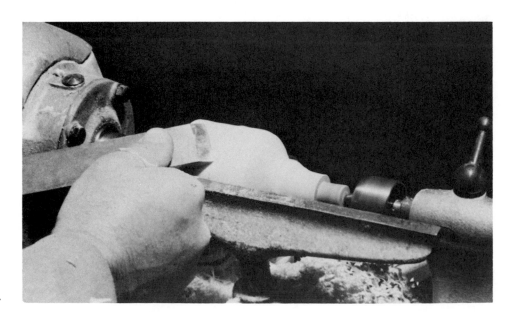

Illus. 49. Planing with the straight-across chisel.

5. The completed profile of the masher head is shown in Illus. 50. The base has been domed with the skew so that it will rock during the mashing process. Glass-paper finish only to avoid food contamination.

Illus. 50. The final profile.

6. Part off with the skew chisel (Illus. 51).

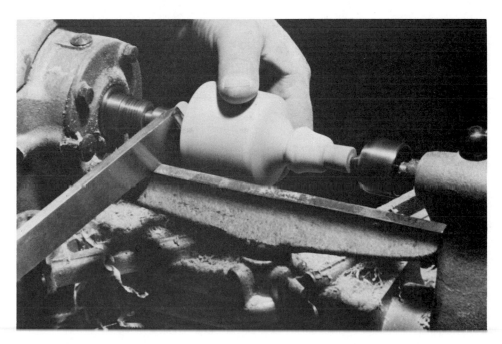

Illus. 51. Parting off.

7. Fix the handle blank between centers and rough down to the largest diameter. A long handrest is required to traverse the straight-across chisel to produce the taper. Turn a tapered spigot at the left-hand side to fit into the masher head (Illus. 52).

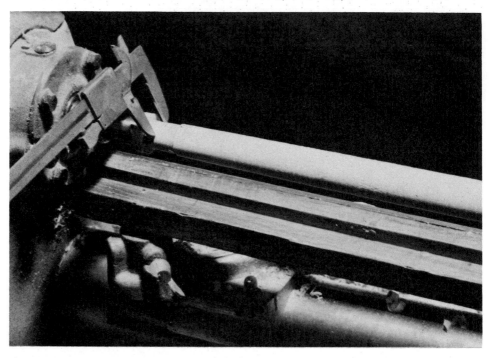

Illus. 52. Check diameter of spigot.

8. Illus. 53 shows the completed handle, with a groove on the right-hand side for a string hanger. Glass-paper only and part off.

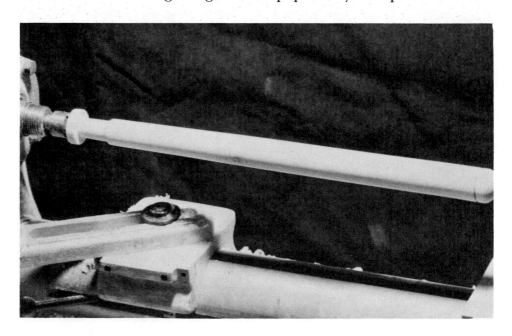

Illus. 53. The handle ready for parting.

11
LACE BOBBIN

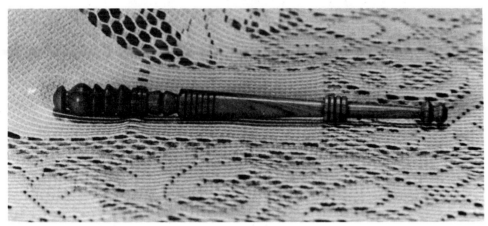

Illus. 54.

WOOD Any straight-grained
  hardwood, particularly exotic
  varieties
  ¼″ × ¼″ × 5½″, allowing
  some waste for the spigot

LATHE ACCESSORIES Spigot chuck with insert
  Revolving center
  Miniature four-pronged
  driving center

OTHER TOOLS Roughing gouge
  Skew chisel, 1¼″
  Spindle gouge
  Beading and parting tool

FINISHING Method 1

DIFFICULTY Grade A

1. Fix the blank between centers, using the miniature four-pronged driving center, and turn a spigot to suit the chuck insert. Remove the workpiece, and then fix it into the spigot-chuck insert (Illus. 55) and rough down to the largest diameter. The work should be very thin and the tailstock should be eased back to reduce pressure.

Illus. 55. The blank with chuck insert.

2. Lace-bobbin patterns are traditional, and vary from area to area; a local crafts museum can be a good source for ideas. All bobbins require a spool to hold the yarn, and a length of usually 1″ should be marked on the tailstock end. Do not rough it out because you first need to work the pattern on the left-hand side (Illus. 56). This example has a "bee's leg" design. Regardless of the design you use, remember that it has to be repeated because lace bobbins are made and sold in pairs.

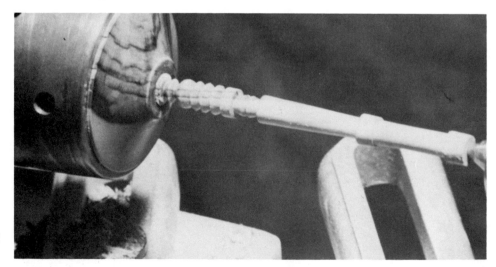

Illus. 56. Work left-hand end first.

3. Working towards the spool, cut the beads on either side of it to leave ¾″ for the spool itself and then glass-paper the whole bobbin to a finish. Finally, reduce the spool to a diameter of ⅛″ and then finish with friction polish only (refer to Method 1 on page 213). You must apply the polish with a soft cloth—not absorbent cotton that will snag and snap the bobbin. Part off, leaving the indent left by the revolving center as a design feature (Illus. 57).

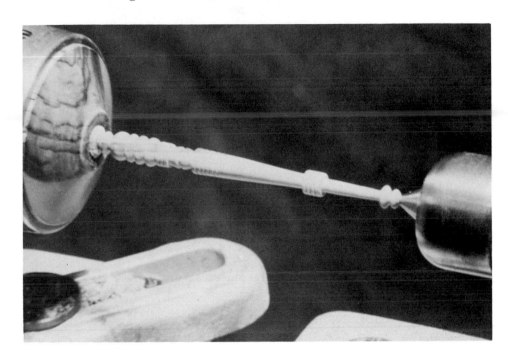

Illus. 57. Note the pleasing taper.

12
KITCHEN-ROLL HOLDER

Illus. 58.

WOOD

Base: suitable disc blank, 6″ in
    diameter and 1″ thick
Spindle: 1¼″ × 1¼″ × 12″

LATHE ACCESSORIES

Screw chuck
Four-pronged driving center
Revolving center
Long handrest

OTHER TOOLS	Superflute bowl gouge
	Roughing gouge
	Skew chisel, 1¼″
	Spindle gouge
	Beading and parting tool
FINISHING	Method 1
DIFFICULTY	Grade A

1. Fix the spindle blank between centers and, using the long hand-rest, rough down to the largest diameter (Illus. 59). Scribe the cylinder ⅝″ from the left-hand side and then turn a spigot of 1″ diameter with a slight taper towards the headstock. Turn to your own design, completely finish, and set aside.

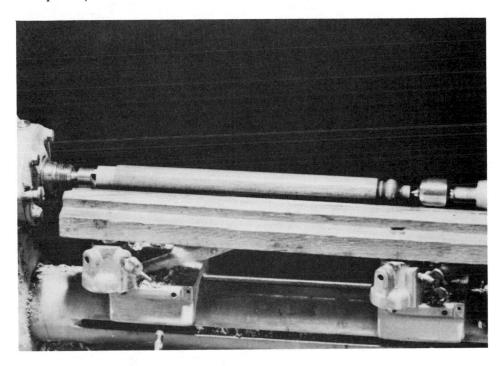

Illus. 59. The spindle.

2. Find the middle of the disc and then drill a hole right through to accept the screw of the screw chuck. You need to make the base first (Illus. 60). True the edges with the Superflute gouge, working from the rims to the middle to avoid breakage, and face the disc, leaving a slightly dished hollow. Finish with abrasive paper on a block, and apply sanding sealer that will help the green baize stick when you apply it later. Reverse the disc on the chuck.

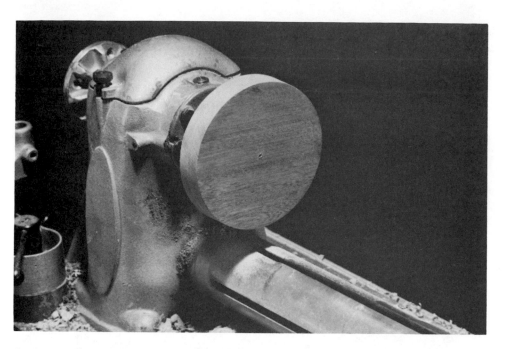

3. True the edge and turn the disc down so that it has a diameter of 5¾″ and is ¾″ thick. Mould the edge, leaving a thin lip, and slightly dish the face (Illus. 61). Completely finish according to Method 1 on page 213 or to your own preference. Now move it to the pillar drill to drill a hole that will accept the spigot.

The finished disc is also an excellent basic design for clockfaces, cheeseboards, and many other useful items.

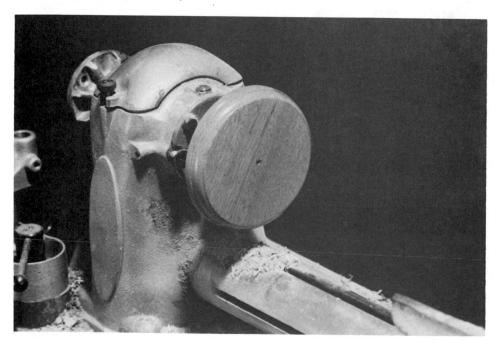

Illus. 61. Complete the moulding.

13
NEEDLECASE

Illus. 62.

WOOD	Yew, ash, or anything suitable 1¾″ × 1¾″ × 5″
LATHE ACCESSORIES	Screw chuck with plywood-backed washer Blacksmith's drill bits, ¾″ and ⅝″ Jacob's chuck Revolving center
OTHER TOOLS	Roughing gouge Skew chisel, 1¼″ Beading and parting tool Spindle gouge Fluted parting tool
FINISHING	Method 1
DIFFICULTY	Grade A

1. You should make the lid first. Mark and drill the wooden blank to a depth of ½″ to accept the chuck screw and then fix between centers. Rough down to a cylinder with the roughing gouge, and square the end with the skew, slightly undercutting from the edge to the center. This will leave a slight dish-shaped depression for a better-fitting lid (Illus. 63).

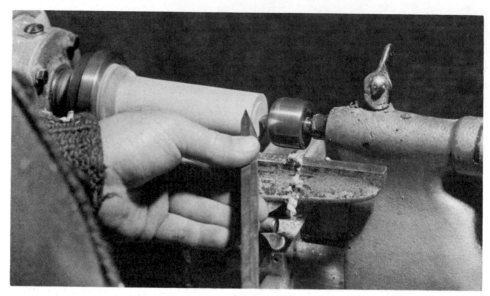

Illus. 63. Dish end of cylinder.

2. Remove the revolving center, replacing it with the Jacob's chuck and ¾″ drill bit. Drill to a depth of ³⁄₁₆″ (Illus. 64). Since both the skew chisel and drill bit produce work that requires no further finishing, only finish and polish the end of the cylinder (see Method 1 on page 213).

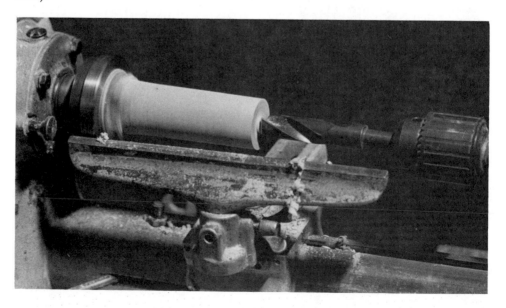

Illus. 64. Drill first hole.

3. Mark the cylinder ⅞″ from the end, and part off using the fluted parting tool (Illus. 65).

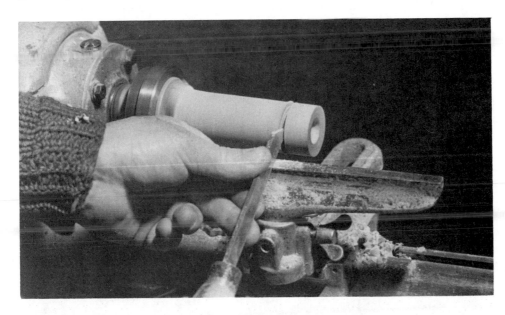

Illus. 65. Part lid.

4. Using the beading and parting tool, mark a groove ¼″ from the end of the cylinder and reduce the cylinder to form a spigot, which will fit into the recess previously drilled in the lid (Illus. 66). Frequently check the measurement of the spigot as you reduce it to avoid overcutting since the lid must have a tight fit. Stop the lathe when offering the lid for sizing against the spigot to avoid damaging the finish.

Illus. 66. Form spigot.

5. Dish the shoulder of the spigot using the skew chisel, undercutting towards the middle as before, and square the cylinder end in preparation for drilling. You can't square the end successfully after drilling because the grain will break away, leaving an untidy finish. Note the skew chisel's angle of presentation (Illus. 67).

Illus. 67. Tidy end grain.

6. Drill through the middle to a depth of 2⅜", using the ⅝" bit (Illus. 68).

Illus. 68. Drill through middle.

7. Stop the lathe and fit the lid, looking for the best grain match (Illus. 69). It should be a tight fit to allow for further chisel work. If the lid appears loose, pack it out with a paper strip.

Illus. 69. Refit lid.

8. Tidy up the cylinder with the roughing gouge to blend in the lid (Illus. 70). Dome the end grain of the lid with the skew chisel.

Illus. 70. True cylinder and lid.

9. Define the base of the box with a groove that is formed by the fluted parting tool 1″ from the face of the screw chuck. Finish with coves and beads to your own design; then glass-paper and polish. After removing the lid, finish the rim and ½″ inside the base. Size the lid, as described for the coin-saver project in the next chapter. Part off and hand-finish the base (Illus. 71). (See Method 1 on page 213.)

Illus. 71. Ready for parting.

14
COIN SAVER

Illus. 72.

WOOD Mahogany or any hardwood
1¾″ × 1¾″ × 4½″

LATHE ACCESSORIES Screw chuck
Revolving center
Jacob's chuck
Saw-toothed machine center bit
  to suit quarters (or pounds)
Saw-toothed machine center bit
  that is ¼″ smaller for lid

OTHER TOOLS	Roughing gouge
	Skew chisel, 1¼″
	Beading and parting tool
	Spindle gouge
FINISHING	Method 1
DIFFICULTY	Grade A

1. Mount the blank on the screw chuck and reduce it to the largest diameter with the roughing gouge, using the revolving center to steady it (Illus. 73). Square the end grain with the skew, slightly undercutting in order to form the base of the lid. This ensures an accurate fit of the base and lid.

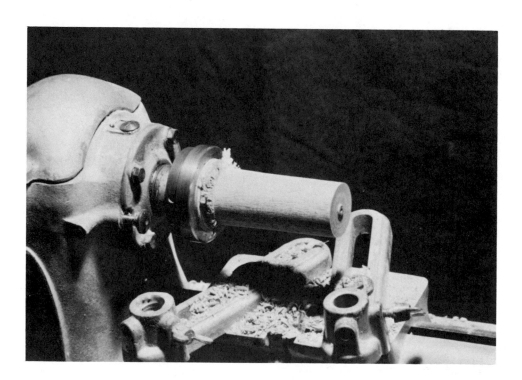

Illus. 73. The prepared blank.

2. Drill out the middle to a depth of ¼″ (Illus. 74), but do not glass-paper because this will enlarge the hole and create a poor fit. Directly apply friction polish and buff to a finish (see Method 1 on page 213). Measure and scribe the cylinder ¾″ from the right-hand end and part off.

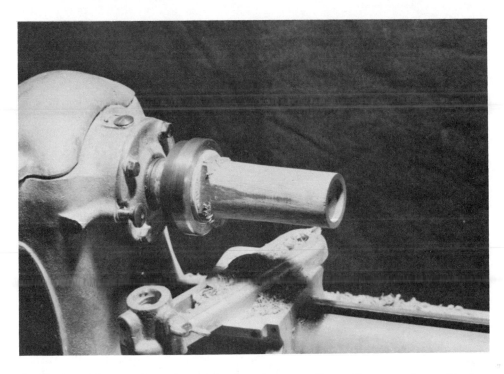

Illus. 74. Inside of lid.

3. Square the end grain with the skew, scribe a line on the cylinder ³⁄₁₆″ from the end, and reduce with the beading and parting tool to the inside diameter of the lid (Illus. 75). Check the measurement frequently to avoid oversizing, and then clean the shoulder with the skew, slightly dishing the cut.

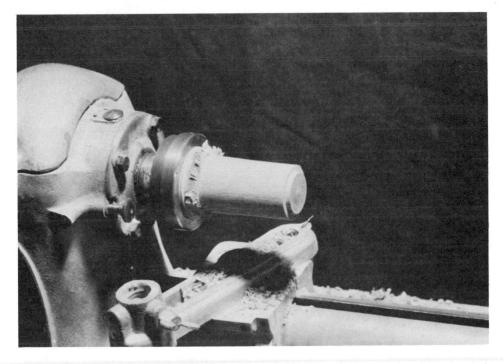

Illus. 75. Lip of box to accept lid.

4. With the 1″ bit, drill through the middle for the coin chamber (Illus. 76). As a guide, a 2½″-deep hole will accommodate $8.00 in quarters (£20 in £1 coins).

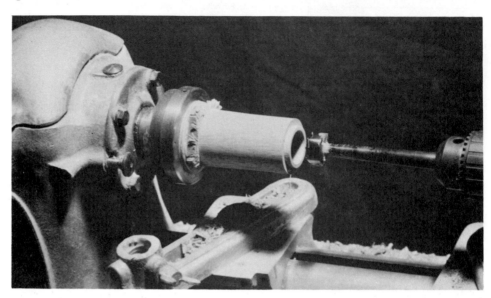

Illus. 76. Drilling out the coin chamber.

5. Push-fit the lid onto the box, looking for the best grain match (Illus. 77). Determine the base of the box and scribe on the cylinder. A convenient measurement is the internal depth plus ¼″. Lightly pass the roughing gouge along the cylinder to blend in the lid and then finish to your own design. Dome the outer edge of the lid with the skew, leaving the middle flat for a single coin to be used as a decoration (see Illus. 72). Glass-paper and finish (see Method 1 on page 213), leaving the space for the coins clear to make gluing easier.

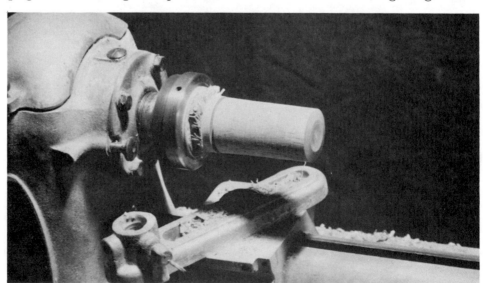

Illus. 77. Replace the lid.

6. To size the lid, remove it, switch on the lathe, quickly push it onto the rim, and then pull it off (Illus. 78). You must do this rapidly to avoid oversizing and to create an excellent fit. After sizing, finish the rim and polish. You don't need to finish the inside of the base beyond ½" inside the rim. Part off and hand-finish the base.

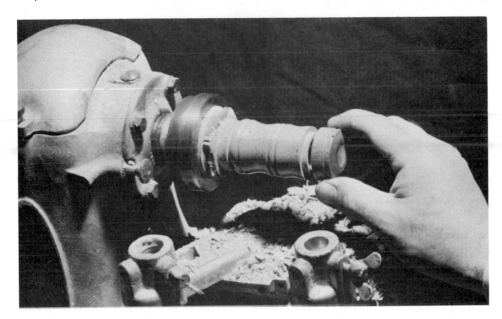

Illus. 78. Sizing the lid.

15
MUSTARD POT

Illus. 79.

WOOD Any hardwood
Pot: 1¾″ × 1¾″ × 3″
Spoon: ⅜″ × ⅜″ × 3″

OTHER MATERIALS Small blue glass pot, 1⁵⁄₁₆″
diameter × 1″

LATHE ACCESSORIES Spigot chuck
Small driving center (for the
spoon)

	Revolving center
	Jacob's chuck
	Saw-toothed machine center
	bit, 1⅜"
OTHER TOOLS	Roughing gouge
	Skew chisel, 1¼"
	Spindle gouge
	Beading and parting tool
	Fluted parting tool
FINISHING	Method 4
DIFFICULTY	Grade B

1. Fix the pot blank between centers, and turn a spigot for the chuck. Insert the piece into the spigot chuck and, using the revolving center to steady it, rough down to the largest diameter. Square the end grain with the skew. You make the lid first. Mark a ring on the end grain 1½" in diameter and then remove the waste inside to a depth of ⅛", slightly doming the interior. Finish the inside completely. Scribe a line 1" from the end of the cylinder (Illus. 80) and part off with the fluted parting tool. This will allow you to form a knob on top of the lid.

Illus. 80. The lid ready for parting.

2. Square the end grain with the skew, and form a rabbet to accept the lid lip (Illus. 81). Drill a hole 1½″ deep with the 1⅜″ bit. Scribe the cylinder 1¹¹⁄₁₆″ from the end to delineate the base.

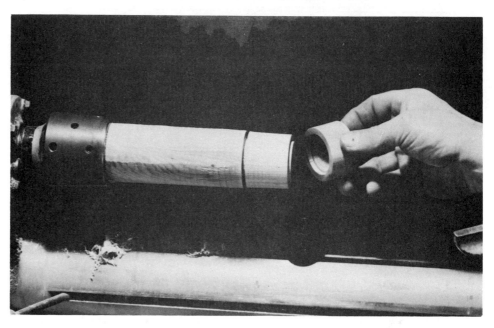

Illus. 81. Fitting the lid.

3. Push-fit the lid and shape the outside of the pot to your own design. Size the lid (as previously described for the coin-saver project), finish with abrasives, and part off (Illus. 82). Use a coat of plastic finish for both the inside and the outside of the pot (see Method 4 on page 214).

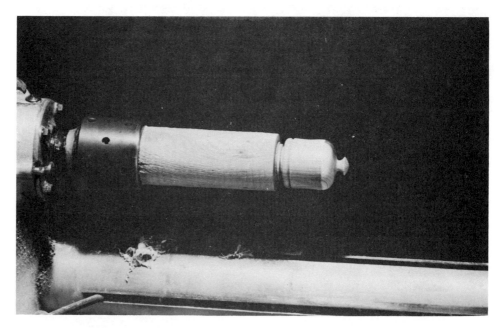

Illus. 82. Ready for parting.

4. To make the spoon, select the small driving center and revolving center, and turn the blank down to the largest diameter. Shape the spoon, remembering that it reaches down through the lid to the base of the glass pot inside (Illus. 83). Hollow out the spoon shape by hand with a firmer gouge after removing the piece from the lathe. Drill the lid so that it can accept the spoon by forming a slot from the hole to the rim.

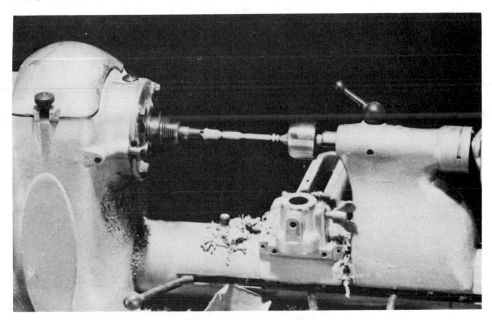

Illus. 83. The spoon.

5. Illus. 84 shows the components ready for assembly.

Illus. 84. Components ready for assembly.

16
ANTIQUE BEEHIVE BOX

Illus. 85.

WOOD   Walnut or exotic hardwood
3″ × 3″ × 5″

LATHE ACCESSORIES   Spigot chuck
Revolving center
Saw-toothed machine center bit

OTHER TOOLS

Roughing gouge
Skew chisel, 1¼″
Beading and parting tool
Spindle gouge
Square-ended scraper
Roundnose scraper

FINISHING　　　　　Method 1

DIFFICULTY　　　　　Grade B

1 Prepare the wood to fit into the spigot chuck (Illus. 86). Using the revolving center to steady the wood, reduce it to the largest diameter with the roughing gouge.

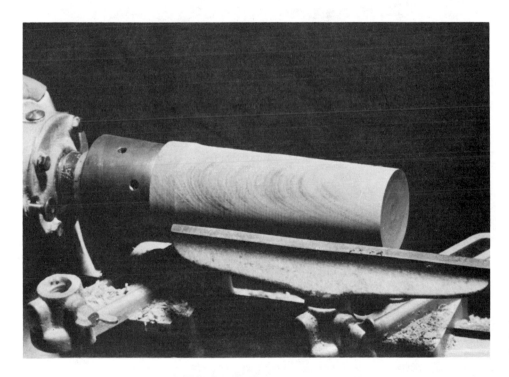

Illus. 86. The prepared blank in the spigot chuck.

2. Make the lid first by scribing the cylinder ⅛″ from the right-hand end; then reduce it to a diameter of 1¾″ with the beading and parting tool. Dish the end of the cylinder with a spindle gouge. Glass-paper and finish according to Method 1 on page 213 or to your own preference (Illus. 87).

3. Mark and scribe the cylinder 1¼″ from the lip and roughly shape the knob (Illus. 88). (You will finish it when you reverse it later.) Part off and then square the end grain with the skew.

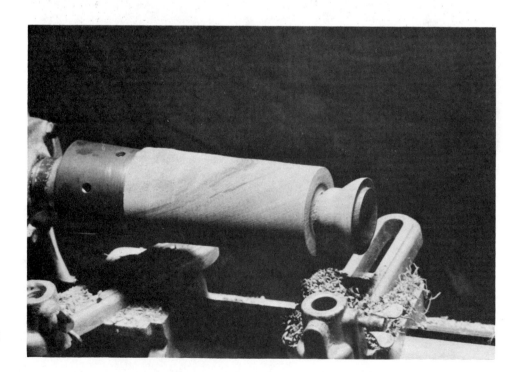

4. Scribe a line 2⅜″ from the right-hand end to delineate the base. Drill out the middle, stepping the hole if a round-interior base is required (Illus. 89).

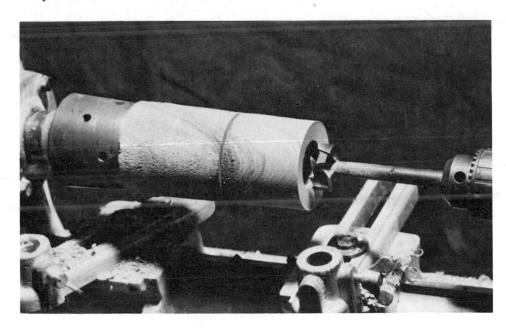

Illus. 89. Drill through the middle.

5. Enlarge the hole with a scraper, leaving the opening a little bit smaller in diameter than the diameter of the lid. Glass-paper the interior, finally enlarging the hole with a scraper to allow a tight push fit for the lid (Illus. 90). Take care not to enlarge the opening when glass-papering.

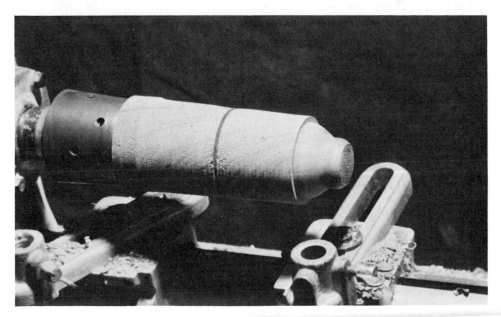

Illus. 90. Push-fit the lid.

6. After first matching the grain, blend in the base to the lid with the roughing gouge (Illus. 91).

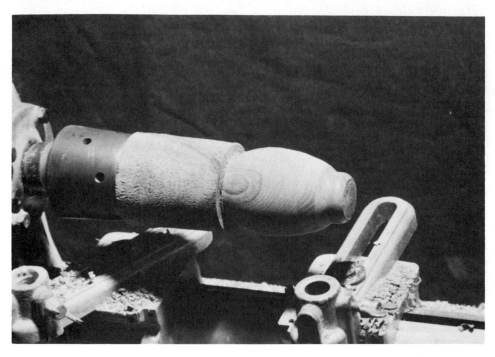

Illus. 91. Blend in lid and box.

7. Shape the outside of the base with a succession of beads. Keep the beads exactly symmetrical for the best effect (Illus. 92). Glass-paper and finish according to Method 1 or to your own preference.

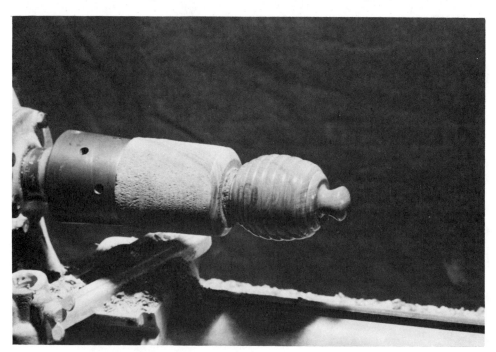

Illus. 92. Note symmetrical beads.

8. Remove the lid and replace it quickly onto the revolving lathe to size it exactly (see Illus. 93 and the instructions for the coin-saver project in Chapter 14). Polish the interior and any visible end grain. Part off and hand-finish the base.

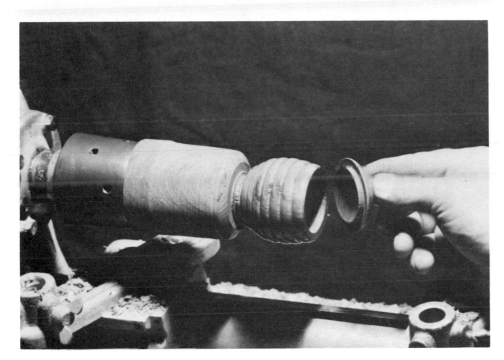

Illus. 93. Sizing the lid.

17
BOX WITH INTEGRAL LID

Illus. 94.

WOOD

Exotic hardwood
3″ × 3″ × 5″

LATHE ACCESSORIES

Spigot chuck
Revolving center
Saw-toothed machine center bit

OTHER TOOLS

Roughing gouge
Skew chisel, 1¼″

Beading and parting tool
Small, domed scraper
Spindle gouge

FINISHING   Method 1

DIFFICULTY   Grade B

1. Prepare the wood for the spigot chuck and produce a spigot 1″ long and 1½″ in diameter. With the beading and parting tool, turn a small lip ³⁄₁₆″ in length at the right-hand end with a slight taper towards the right. Glass-paper the lip and finish (Illus. 95). Part off.

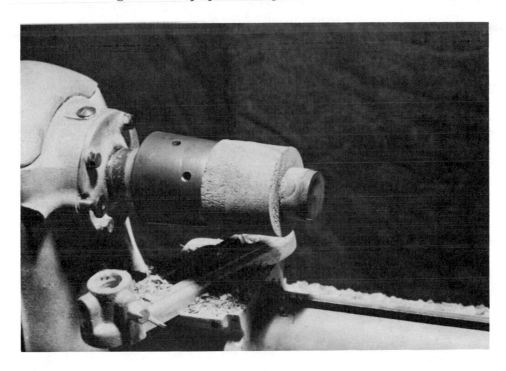

Illus. 95. Spigot and finished lip.

2. Square the end grain with the skew, and drill through the middle to a diameter smaller than that of the lid. Scrape out the interior of the box and then glass-paper, taking care not to enlarge the opening. Push-fit the lid (Illus. 96).

3. As with the beehive box in Chapter 16, shape the lid and box together, glass-paper, and then finish according to Method 1 on page 213 or your own preference (Illus. 97). Remove the lid and size the opening, leaving a loose fit by removing waste with the scraper from the body of the box. Polish the box interior and any exposed end grain. Part off and then hand-finish the base.

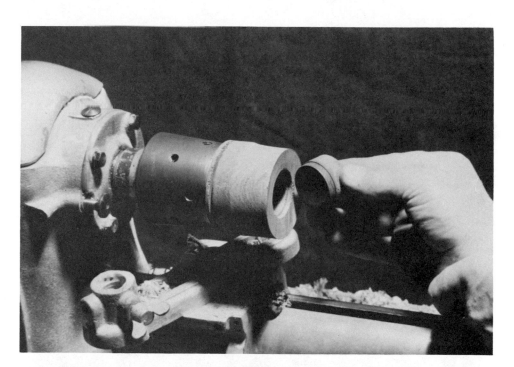

Illus. 96. Push-fit the lid.

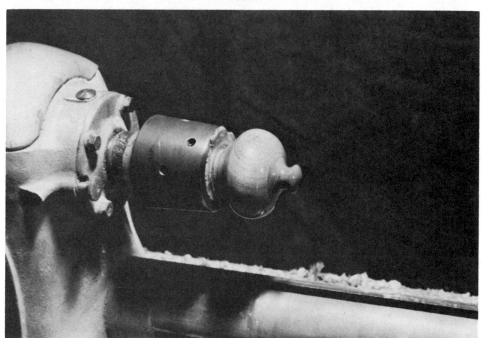

Illus. 97. The finished exterior.

18
PEPPER POT

Illus. 98.

WOOD Yew, ash, or anything suitable
1¾″ × 1¾″ × 5″

OTHER MATERIALS Plastic lid for pot base

LATHE ACCESSORIES Screw chuck with plywood-
    backed washer
Drill bit to suit diameter of
    plastic lid
Saw-toothed machine center
    bit, 1¼″
Revolving center

	Jacob's chuck
	Plug to suit base hole
OTHER TOOLS	Roughing gouge
	Skew chisel, 1¼″
	Beading and parting tool
	Spindle gouge
	Fluted parting tool
FINISHING	Method 1
DIFFICULTY	Grade B

1. Rough down to a cylinder using the roughing gouge with the revolving center for support, and square the end grain with the skew (Illus. 99). This will form the base of the pot, which should be slightly dished to prevent rocking when placed on a flat surface.

Illus. 99. Square end grain.

2. Fit the Jacob's chuck and the 1¼″ saw-toothed bit, and countersink the base to a depth of twice the thickness of the lip on the lid (Illus. 100). This will ensure that the lid is suitably buried, preventing the pot from rocking.

3. Measure the diameter of the lid and select a suitable drill bit to drill out the middle to a depth of 3⅛″ (Illus. 101).

Illus. 100. Drill hole for lid.

Illus. 101. Bore through pepper chamber.

4. Delineate the top of the pot by cutting a groove with the fluted parting tool 1″ from the face of the screw chuck, and shape the outside of the cylinder to your own design. Finish and polish the rabbets in the base, but finish the outside of the cylinder with garnet

paper only; do not apply polish at this stage. (See Method 1 on page 213.) Part off (Illus. 102).

Illus. 102. Ready for parting.

5. Select a plug with a long taper to give adequate support inside the bore and then fit it to the screw chuck (Illus. 103). To make your own plug, follow the instructions in Chapter 44.

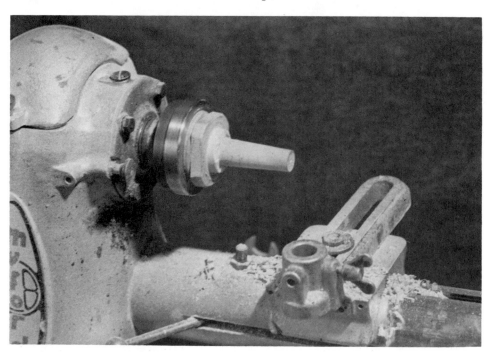

Illus. 103. Plug fitted to screw chuck.

6. Ease the pot onto the plug so that it fits snugly and then switch it on. Any eccentricity will immediately be seen. If necessary, stop the lathe and make the adjustment to ensure that the work will run true. Dome the top using the long corner of the skew chisel (Illus. 104).

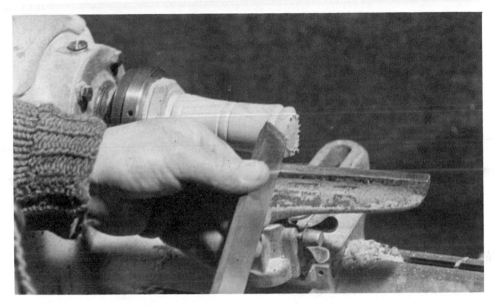

Illus. 104. Doming with the skew.

7. Before removing the work from the lathe for drilling the top holes, mark a circle in pencil with its diameter inside the diameter of the pepper chamber (Illus. 105). Remove the work and, on a bench drill, drill the holes for dispensing the pepper. You can make a matching salt pot the same way, but drill only one central hole at this stage.

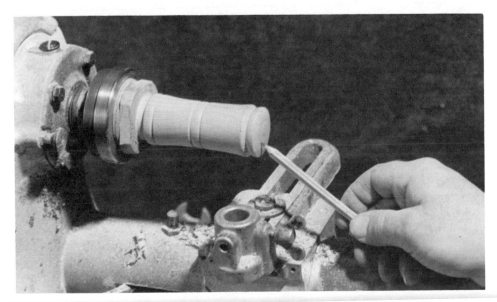

Illus. 105. Mark for top holes.

8. Replace the work on the plug, lining it up as accurately as possible. A slight misalignment is permissible here because no further tool work is required. Finish and polish according to Method 1 on page 213 (Illus. 106); then fit the plastic lid.

Illus. 106. Finished pot.

9. If you don't have a saw-toothed bit that is large enough to produce the recess at the base, you can use a scraper instead (Illus. 107). Work from the middle to the edge, removing small shavings only to prevent the work from being forced off the screw chuck.

Illus. 107. Scraping the counterbore recess.

19 CIRCULAR PICTURE FRAME

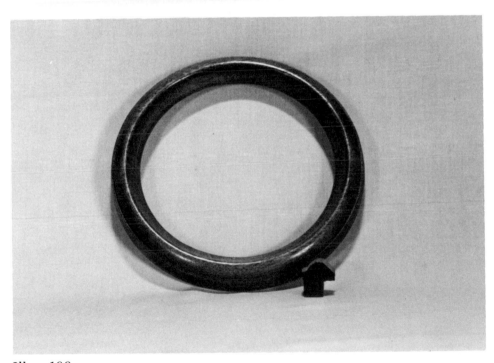

Illus. 108.

WOOD

Use a suitably seasoned blank sawn to a 7½″ diameter with a thickness of 1″.

Any stable wood is acceptable, but one surface must be planed flat for accurate chucking.

LATHE ACCESSORIES	Faceplate for outboard turning, 6″ in diameter
	Use a homemade jig from a planed wooden disc 6⅞″ in diameter and ¾″ thick. The jig is drilled with two holes 6½″ apart at 12 and 6 o'clock.
OTHER TOOLS	Superflute gouge
	Straight-across scraper
	Narrow scraper
FINISHING	Method 1 or 4
DIFFICULTY	Grade B

1. For a 6″-diameter picture, the outside diameter of the blank is reduced to 7″. Fix the blank to the faceplate by the inner set of holes to prevent the screw holes from damaging the frame moulding. True the edge with the Superflute gouge to the 7″ diameter (Illus. 109).

Illus. 109. True the edge.

2. The part of the disc facing outward becomes the back of the finished frame. Face off this surface to a thickness of ⅞″, producing a

good finish on the outer ¾″ of the rim (Illus. 110). For two finishing alternatives, see Method 1 on page 213 and Method 4 on page 214.

Illus. 110. Finish on outer rim.

3. Scribe two rings on the face, one 6″ in diameter and the other 4¾″ in diameter (Illus. 111).

Illus. 111. Scribe two rings on the face.

4. With a scraper, remove the waste between the rings to a depth of ⅜″ (see Illus. 112 and 113). This will produce the rabbet for the glass, picture, and backing card.

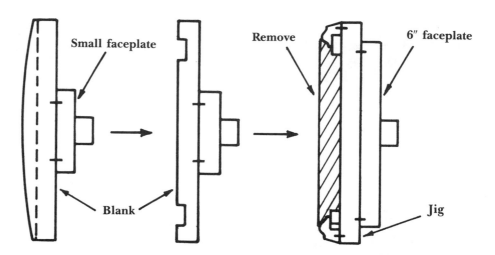

Illus. 112. Sequence of waste removal.

Small faceplate

Remove

6″ faceplate

Blank

Jig

Illus. 113. Remove waste between lines.

5. Remove the disc from the lathe. Fix the jig onto a faceplate that is 6″ in diameter. Fit the frame centrally onto the jig, screwing through the jig into the outer edge of the frame with No. 6 screws, which protrude no more than ½″ into the frame.

Tidy the rim to center it and form a slight taper from back to front to produce a more aesthetic profile with less bulk. Mark a ring 5″ in diameter on the face and remove the waste inside this line with a small scraper, cutting through to the jig behind. Note the screw holes left from the first operation (Illus. 114).

Illus. 114. Frame reversed onto jig with waste removed.

6. Form the frame profile to your own design (see Illus. 115 and 116).

Illus. 115. Form the frame profile.

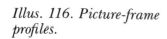

Illus. 116. Picture-frame profiles.

7. Select a picture for the frame (Illus. 117). Cut the glass, picture, and backing card to suit the rabbet and then affix the picture hangers.

Illus. 117. Suitable subject for framing.

20
CIGAR HOLDER

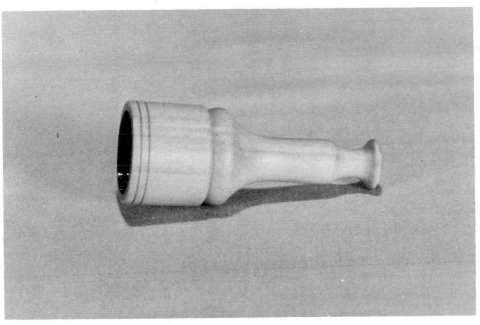

Illus. 118.

WOOD

Any close-grained, nontoxic hardwood
$1\frac{1}{4}'' \times 1\frac{1}{4}'' \times 3\frac{1}{2}''$

LATHE ACCESSORIES

Four-pronged driving center, small
Four-pronged driving center, large
Revolving center
Jacob's chuck
Drills to suit cigar diameter
Drill bit, $\frac{1}{8}''$
Plug for largest hole

OTHER TOOLS	Roughing gouge
	Skew chisel, 1¼″
	Beading and parting tool
	Spindle gouge
FINISHING	Method 4
DIFFICULTY	Grade B

1. Rough down the workpiece to the largest diameter and square the end grain with the skew. With the larger bit, drill out the end to a depth of 1″ to accept the cigar (Illus. 119). A drill with a point is preferable because it acts as a guide for the second hole.

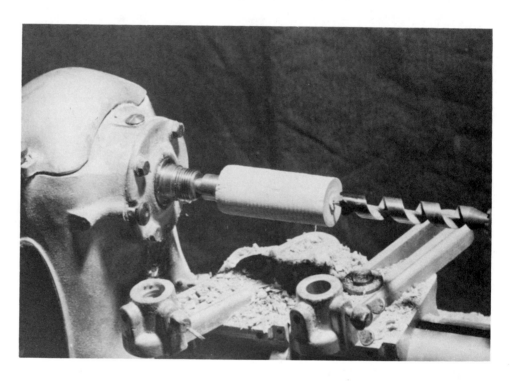

Illus. 119. Drilling the first hole.

2. Using the previous hole as a guide, follow with the ⅛″ drill to a depth of 3″ from the lip. This produces the air hole (Illus. 120). Some wandering of the bit is inevitable, so remove the piece and cut off ⅝″ from the left-hand end to allow for any inaccuracy.

3. Measure and mark the depth of the large hole on the outside of the cylinder; then remount in the lathe with a plug in the larger hole of the cylinder and a miniature four-pronged driving center at the

headstock (Illus. 121). (If you want to make your own plug, see the instructions in Chapter 44.)

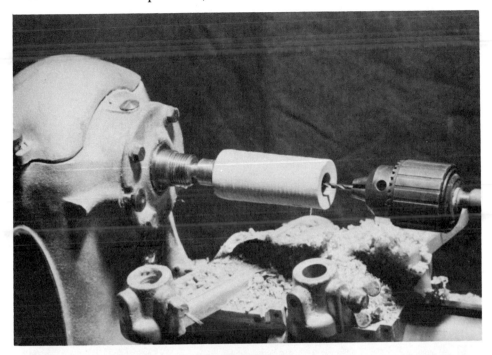

Illus. 120. Drilling the air hole.

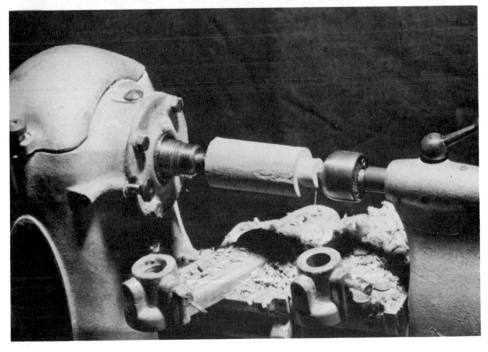

Illus. 121. The plug in the larger hole.

4. Shape the mouthpiece, stem, and holder and then use glass paper. You can leave the holder unfinished or use a plastic coating. As an alternative, you can use beeswax, but leave the mouthpiece clear

(Illus. 122). Finally, part with the skew chisel, remembering to proceed carefully since the mouthpiece is hollow.

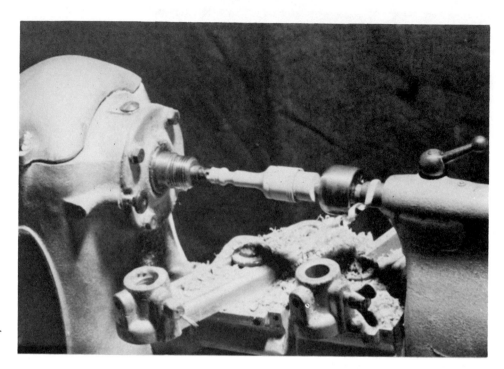

Illus. 122. Finish to your own design.

21
APPLES AND PEARS

Illus. 123.

WOOD

Use anything suitable—
   laburnum is especially
   attractive.
$3'' \times 3'' \times 12''$

LATHE ACCESSORIES

Spigot chuck
Revolving center
Small driving center

OTHER TOOLS	Roughing gouge
	Skew chisel, 1¼″
	Spindle gouge
	Beading and parting tool
	Fluted parting tool
FINISHING	Method 1
DIFFICULTY	Grade B

1. Apples and pears at first seem very easy to make, but creating realistic-looking fruit out of wood is actually very difficult. Study some real fruit before working on the lathe to establish the flowing lines that are required.

Place the workpiece in the spigot chuck. Using the revolving center to steady it, rough down to the largest diameter (Illus. 124). The 12″ piece allows you to produce several pieces of fruit in one session.

Illus. 124. Rough down to the largest diameter.

2. Here are the instructions for making the apple. Mark and scribe the cylinder ¼″ longer than the diameter. Make a relieving cut with the gouge at this point to allow access to the base of the apple (Illus. 125). This cut also forms the top of the pear, which you should make next to eliminate waste.

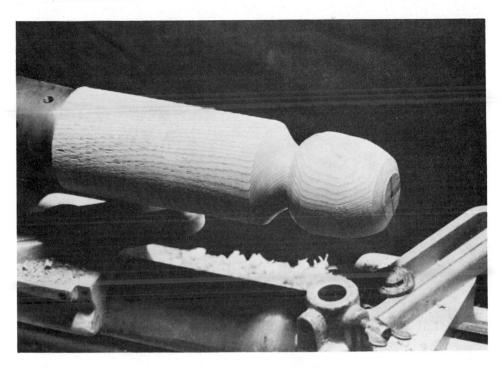

Illus. 125. Note the relieving cut forming the start of the pear.

3. Round the right-hand end of the cylinder with the spindle gouge. Undercut the base with the fluted parting tool, glass-paper, and then finish according to Method 1 on page 213 or to your own preference. Slightly undercut the base when parting to make sure that the apple will be stable (Illus. 126).

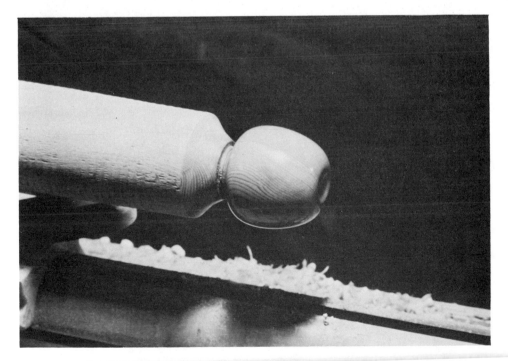

Illus. 126. The completed apple.

4. Here are the instructions for the pear. Scribe the cylinder approximately 3¼″ from the top of the previously made taper and turn the pear shape (Illus. 127). Undercut the base as before, and also dish the top to accept a stalk. Glass-paper, finish according to Method 1 or your own preference, and then part off.

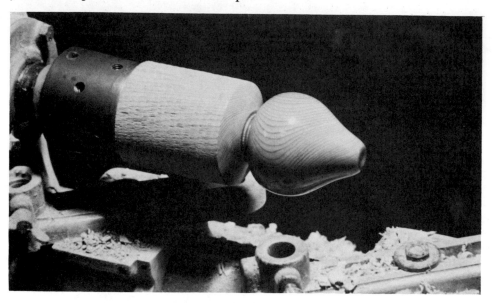

Illus. 127. Form the pear.

5. When you have completed a number of apples and pears, select some waste lumber (preferably a dark color), fix between the small driving center and the revolving center, and then turn a small stalk (Illus. 128). After first making a hole with a bradawl, glue the stalk into the depression at the top of the fruit.

Illus. 128. The stalk.

22
LOG TABLE LAMP

Illus. 129.

WOOD

A log section, complete with
  bark, that is well seasoned
  and free from splits
10″/12″ long

LATHE ACCESSORIES

Four-pronged driving center
Revolving center
5⁄16″ auger and hollow dead
  center, or drill bit with
  morse-taper shank

OTHER TOOLS	Roughing gouge Skew chisel, 1¼″ Spindle gouge Beading and parting tool Fluted parting tool
FINISHING	Method 1 for exposed grain Sanding sealer for bark
DIFFICULTY	Grade B

1. Select the log very carefully to make sure that it is free from splits (Illus. 130). Using a low-lathe speed because of the irregular shape, square both ends with the skew chisel.

Illus. 130. Check log for splits.

2. As long as the log is sound, there is no reason to reject a log with branch projections, such as the one in Illus. 131. You can carefully trim the branch projections with the roughing gouge on a low-lathe speed, and they will produce interesting surface features.

Using an auger or a drill bit, drill a hole to within 1″ of the driving center to accept the cable and the electric bulb holder. Replace the drill bit with the revolving center and shape to your own design, being careful to retain as much bark as possible. Finish the exposed material below the bark by hand to avoid damage, using a toothbrush for the bark. Apply sanding sealer all over; then friction-polish and wax the exposed grain only (see Method 1 on page 213).

On the pillar drill, drill an exit hole for the wire in the side of the base and a 1″-diameter hole in the base itself to meet the first hole drilled on the lathe. This will enable you to pull the wire through and turn it into the exit hole, without fouling the base, but allowing it to stand perfectly square. Screw in the electric fitting and assemble.

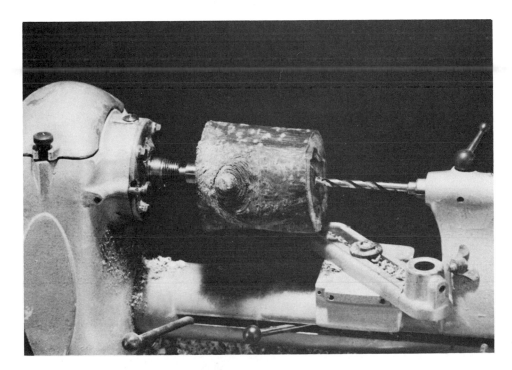

Illus. 131. Drill cable hole.

23
EGGCUP

Illus. 132.

WOOD

Any suitable wood
2″ × 2″ × 10″ for a set of four
  eggcups

LATHE ACCESSORIES

Spigot chuck
Revolving center
Plug

OTHER TOOLS

Roughing gouge
Skew chisel, 1¼″
Spindle gouge

Beading and parting tool
Fluted parting tool
Goblet gouge
Spindle gouge, ¼"

FINISHING   Method 4

DIFFICULTY   Grade B

1. Prepare the blank for the spigot chuck; then insert and rough down to the largest diameter. Square the end grain with the skew, and mark the end of the cylinder with a 1½"-diameter circle. To obtain a better internal finish, remove waste with a goblet gouge to the profile of an egg (Illus. 133).

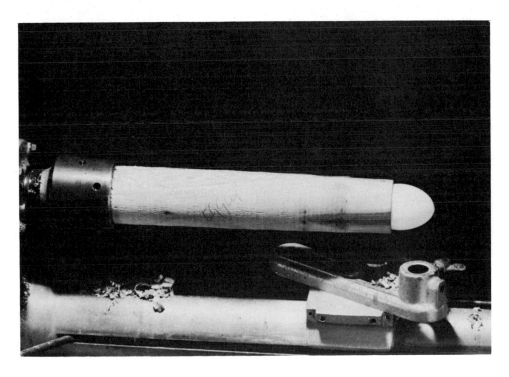

Illus. 133. Use egg for sizing.

2. Measure 2" from the face of the cylinder, and scribe a line for the base with the fluted parting tool. Also mark the stem and cup base and then insert the plug into the cavity (Illus. 134). Turn to your own design and part with the fluted parting tool to minimize waste. Fit a screw eye into the base for hanging while applying plastic-coat finish according to Method 4 on page 214.

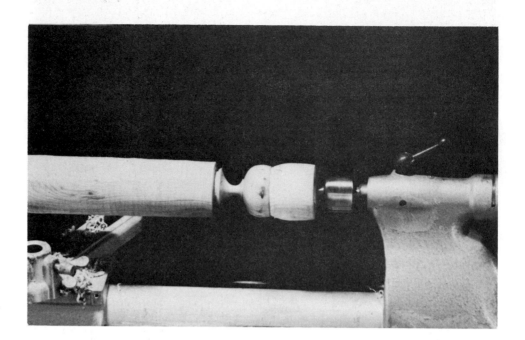

Illus. 134. The plug in position.

24
BABY'S RATTLE

Illus. 135.

WOOD	Sycamore, beech, or any other nontoxic wood 1½″ × 1½″ × 8½″
LATHE ACCESSORIES	Four-pronged driving center Revolving center
OTHER TOOLS	Roughing gouge Skew chisels, 1¼″ and ½″ Spindle gouge Beading and parting tool
FINISHING	Abrasives only
DIFFICULTY	Grade B

1. Fix the blank between centers and rough down to the largest diameter. Scribe three beads as follows:

    a. Measure 2″ from the left-hand end of the cylinder and scribe a line.

    b. Scribe the next lines at 2¼″, 2¾″, 3″, 3½″, and 3¾″.

Scribe a line at 5½″ from the left-hand side to delineate the handle (Illus. 136).

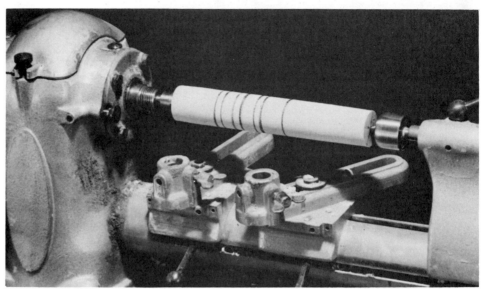

Illus. 136. Scribe bead lines.

2. With the beading and parting tool, reduce the waste in between the beads to a depth equal to the width of the beads. Form the beads and then finish with abrasives, further reducing the waste in between to a diameter of ⅞″ (Illus. 137).

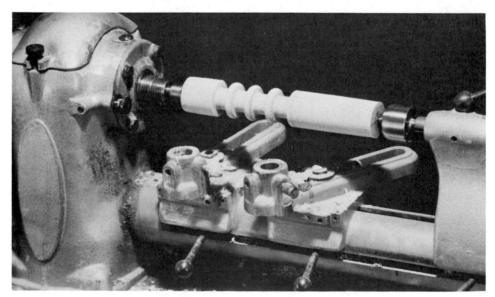

Illus. 137. Reduce waste between beads.

3. With the ½″ skew, undercut the beads from both the left- and right-hand sides (Illus. 138). Glass-paper the rings to a finish before cutting right through.

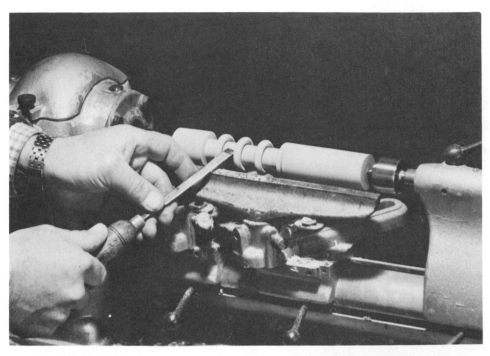

Illus. 138. Cut through with small skew chisel.

4. Shape the handle (to fit a baby's hand) and the head, forming holding pips at the headstock and tailstock (Illus. 139).

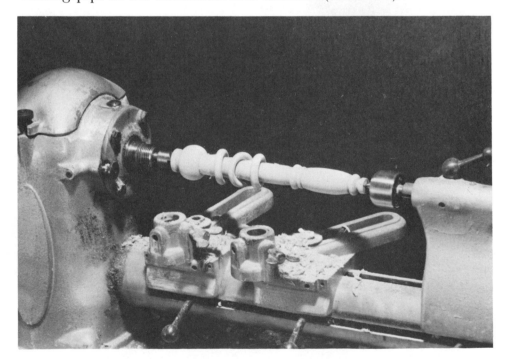

Illus. 139. Shape head and handle.

5. Reduce the spindle below the beads to a ½″ diameter to allow plenty of room for the beads to move and produce a good rattling sound (Illus. 140). As you reduce the spindle, it's a good idea to tape the beads because the centrifugal force will make them fly about. Finish only with abrasives and then part off.

This item makes a nice gift for *someone else's* baby.

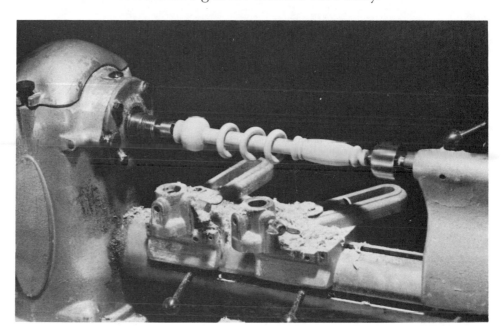

Illus. 140. Reduce central spindle.

25
NAPKIN RINGS

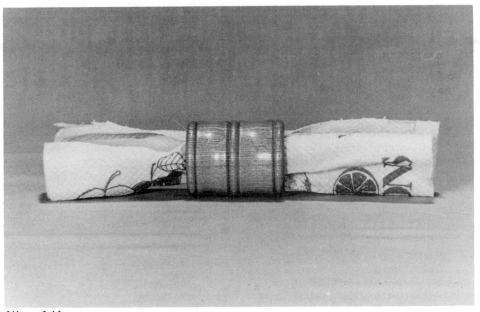

Illus. 141.

WOOD
Anything suitable
$2'' \times 2'' \times 2\frac{1}{4}''$

LATHE ACCESSORIES
Coil chuck or something
  similar, with expanding
  wooden spigot chuck and
  screw-chuck insert
Machine center bit, $1\frac{1}{4}''$
Four-pronged center
Revolving center
Mandrel

OTHER TOOLS
Roughing gouge

	Beading and parting tool
	Spindle gouge
FINISHING	Method 1 or 4
DIFFICULTY	Grade B

1. Support the workpiece on the screw-chuck insert, using the revolving center to steady it (Illus. 142). Rough down to the largest diameter.

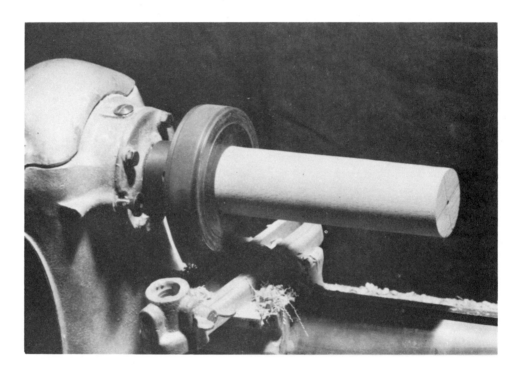

Illus. 142. Insert the work into the chuck.

2. With the 1¼″ bit, drill out the middle for one napkin ring only (Illus. 143). Part off prior to fitting it to the expanding chuck.

3. Fit the expanding spigot chuck to the lathe (Illus. 144).

4. Push-fit the napkin-ring blank onto the spigot chuck and tighten the ring (Illus. 145). Scribe the outside of the cylinder with the beading and parting tool for beads and coves to your own design.

5. Shape the outside and, for a professional-looking finish, round the lip and glass-paper to a finish (Illus. 146). Reverse the workpiece in the chuck and form the lip on the other end. Glass-paper to a finish.

6. Remove the chuck and fit the four-pronged driving center, the revolving center, and the tapered mandrel (Illus. 147). Finish the napkin ring completely, applying friction polish by hand for the inside. See Method 1 on page 213 or Method 4 on page 214 for finishing alternatives.

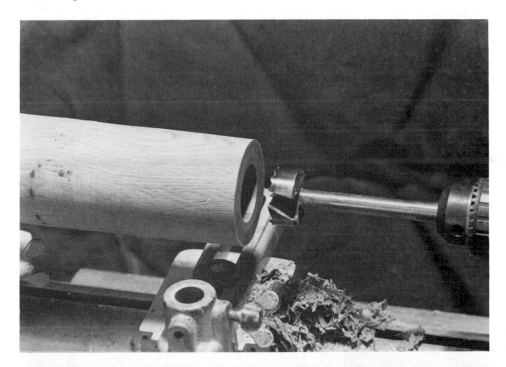

Illus. 143. Drill for one ring only.

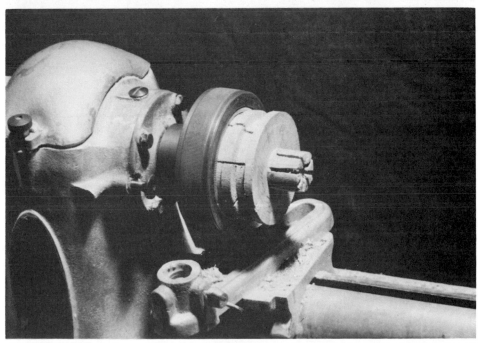

Illus. 144. The expanding spigot chuck in position.

Illus. 145. The ring held by the spigot.

Illus. 146. Note the rounded lip.

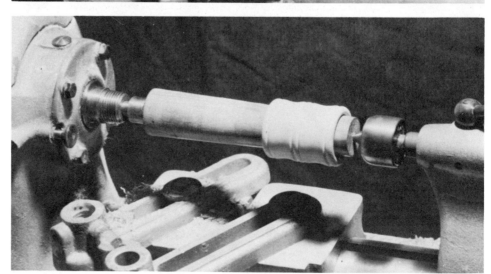

Illus. 147. The tapered mandrel.

26
BOWL—FACEPLATE METHOD

Illus. 148.

WOOD

Wet elm, unseasoned blank, or
    seasoned bowl blank
2½″ thick and 10″ in diameter

LATHE ACCESSORIES

4″-diameter faceplate for
    outboard turning
Four screws, ⅜″, to penetrate
    the wood

OTHER TOOLS	Superflute bowl gouge
	Straight-across scraper
	Beading and parting tool
FINISHING	Method 1 or 2
DIFFICULTY	Grade B

1. Refer to Illus. 149. Carefully examine the square bowl blank to establish the direction of the annual rings. The rings tend to straighten during seasoning. You can make a more stable finished bowl if you remove the waste following the curvature of the rings (a).

Cut the blank into a disc and center the faceplate. Insert two gauge-12 screws in the direction of the grain and two at right angles to it, penetrating the blank surface by no more than ⅜″. Do not drill pilot holes for the screws; it's very easy to drill too far, leaving holes on the inside of the bowl bottom. Merely hammer the screws in to start the threads and then screw home (b).

When checking a seasoned bowl blank, you will probably find it to be oval in shape with the two screw holes in the direction of the grain still in the same place. Shrinkage will probably have moved the other two holes, so more holes will be required, although you can turn the blank even if it's held by only two screws. Finish the base of the bowl by planing before affixing the faceplate (c).

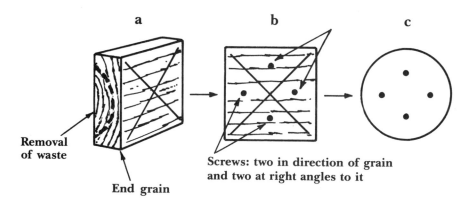

Illus. 149. Fixing the faceplate.

2. The wet bowl blank is now ready for turning to produce a disc for storing and seasoning (Illus. 150).

3. Shape the outside to a rough profile (Illus. 151).

4. Hollow out the middle of the bowl to a thickness of 1″, following the outside profile (Illus. 152).

Illus. 150. Wet bowl blank.

Illus. 151. Shape the outside to rough profile.

Illus. 152. Hollow out bowl.

5. The roughed out blank is now ready for removal and storing. Note on the back the date it was turned (Illus. 153).

Illus. 153. Finished wet blank.

6. The seasoned blank after 6 months' storage is shown in Illus. 154. Note the oval shape.

Illus. 154. Seasoned blank after storage.

7. Turn the outside first and then finish with abrasive paper (Illus. 155).

Illus. 155. Turn the outside first.

8. Hollow out the inside of the bowl (Illus. 156).

Illus. 156. Hollowing with Superflute.

9. Mark a lip on the outside of the bowl in pencil and then turn a bead with the beading and parting tool and the straight-across scraper (Illus. 157). Finish completely, remove, and then fill the screw holes with wooden plugs or a filler. If you cover the base with sanding sealer and allow it to dry for 10 minutes, you can stick on green baize without it peeling off later. For finishing alternatives, see Method 1 or 2 on page 213.

Illus. 157. Finish with a bead.

27
BOWL WITH BARK LIP

Illus. 158.

WOOD   Use found logs with bark, but
                         make sure they are not
                         rotten inside.

LATHE ACCESSORIES   Pin chuck
                         Bowl chuck
                         Pillar drill

OTHER TOOLS   Superflute bowl gouge
                         Square-ended scraper

V-section wooden block support for round work on pillar drill

FINISHING

Instructions included here

DIFFICULTY

Grade C

1. Cut a suitable slice from your log, first checking to see that it is free from old nails or wire (Illus. 159). A metal detector is an invaluable accessory for checking found logs.

Illus. 159. Trim your log to size.

2. Using a pillar drill, prepare the log to accept a pin chuck in accordance with the manufacturer's instructions (Illus. 160).

3. Illus. 161 shows the log and pin chuck. Note that this work is carried out on the outboard end of the lathe.

4. With the Superflute gouge, turn down to the largest diameter (Illus. 162). You need to take special care when starting the lathe because of the irregularly shaped workpiece. It tends to cause heavy vibration, which eases as you bring the outside to a cylinder with the gouge.

5. Turn a spigot to accept a homemade or manufacturer's bowl chuck (Illus. 163).

6. Reverse the workpiece, fitting it into the bowl chuck. Check to see if it is running true, removing any waste as required. Delineate the

Illus. 161. Pin chuck ready for insertion.

outer diameter of the bowl with a scraper and begin removing the central waste (Illus. 164).

7. Continue hollowing out the middle of the bowl with the Super-flute gouge, leaving a ring of bark on the bowl lip (Illus. 165). If the

Illus. 162. Gradual removal of the outer bark.

Illus. 163. The spigot prepared for the bowl chuck.

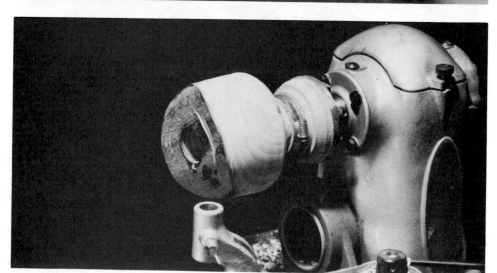

Illus. 164. Note mark left by scraper on face of log.

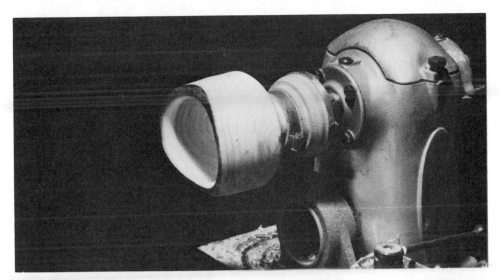

Illus. 165. Note ring of bark.

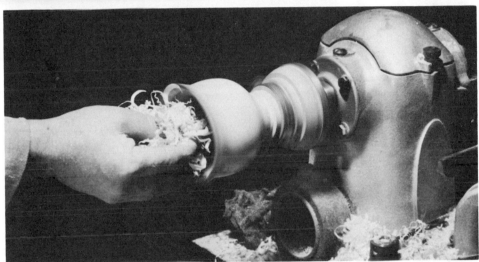

Illus. 166. Burnishing the inside.

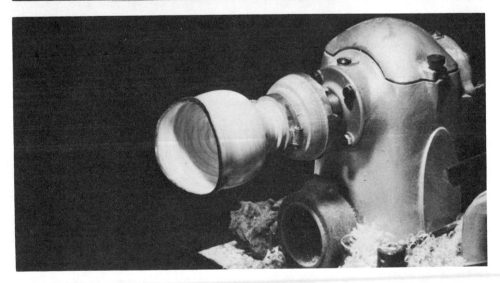

Illus. 167. The finished bowl.

log is very wet, you must leave the bowl for a while "in the rough" to season. When the bowl is adequately seasoned, proceed with the finishing instructions that follow.

8. Shape the outside of the bowl with the Superflute gouge and delineate the base. Finish the inside with abrasive paper, being very careful when inserting your fingers because of the irregularly shaped lip (Illus. 166). You can leave the sides very thin and translucent; but if too much heat is built up by glass-papering, cracks will soon appear.

9. Finish the bowl with Danish oil, inside and out, and part off, dishing the cut at the base to ensure that the bowl will stand without rocking (Illus. 167). Cover with baize as required.

28
BOWL WITH CERAMIC INSERT

Illus. 168.

WOOD   Suitably seasoned bowl blank,
                            any diameter 1½″ deep

OTHER MATERIALS   Tile insert

LATHE ACCESSORIES   Small faceplate or chuck for
                            outboard turning

OTHER TOOLS   Superflute bowl gouge
                            Straight-across scraper

FINISHING DIFFICULTY

Method 1

Grade C

1. Fix the bowl blank to the chuck and turn to finish the outside shape (Illus. 169).

Illus. 169. Shape outside of blank.

2. Mark the outer diameter of the tile in the middle of the bowl, as well as another circle ¼″ larger in diameter outside it (Illus. 170). This will delineate the base frame, which is raised above the bowl surface to accept the tile.

Illus. 170. Mark edges of base frame.

3. Hollow out the edges of the bowl to the outer rim of the base frame (Illus. 171); then finish with abrasives. Apply sanding sealer, friction polish, and wax to the outside and inside of the bowl, leaving the area inside the circle unfinished at this stage (see Method 1 on page 213).

Illus. 171. Hollow out bowl to base-frame edge.

4. Remove the waste from the inner ring with the scraper (Illus. 172). The tile looks better if you leave it just a bit higher than the rim of the surrounding wood.

Illus. 172. Remove waste from inner ring.

5. Glue in the tile with a flexible tile adhesive (Illus. 173), finish the bottom with abrasives, and then apply sanding sealer. Leave it to dry for 10 minutes and then stick on self-adhesive baize.

Illus. 173. Glue in tile.

29
EGG TIMER

Illus. 174.

WOOD
Any type of hardwood discs, 4½" in diameter and 1" thick
Spindles: three pieces, 5½" × ⅝" × ⅝"

OTHER MATERIALS
Hourglass (for this project, one that is 4¾", timing approximately 5 minutes)

LATHE ACCESSORIES
Combination chuck with screw and collet fittings
Miniature four-pronged center

	Electric drill/pillar drill
	Drill bit, ¼″
OTHER TOOLS	Superflute bowl gouge
	Roughing gouge
	Skew chisel, 1¼″
	Beading and parting tool
	Straight-across scraper
	Narrow scraper
FINISHING	Method 1
DIFFICULTY	Grade C

1. Since the hourglass is reversed in use, it does not have a true base. Any screw holes used in chucking would therefore show if you turned it using conventional methods. To overcome this problem, you need to use a collet chuck and leave the ring into which the collet fits as part of the final design (Illus. 175).

To make the first disc, select the screw-chuck assembly of the combination chuck and affix the blank, making sure that the screw does not penetrate the other side of the disc. A depth of ½″ is ideal and a plywood washer placed between the disc and chuck will also help. Turn the disc to 4″, face the surface with the Superflute gouge, and form the recess for the collet chuck with a small scraper. Completely finish, using Method 1 on page 213 or any method you prefer. Make another disc the same way.

Illus. 175. Recess for collet chuck.

2. Remove the screw chuck and reverse the work, fitting it to the collet assembly by the previously turned groove. True the edge as necessary, cutting a slight taper from the back to the front, and face the disc. Enlarge the central hole left by the screw chuck with a small scraper to accept the projection on the base of the hourglass (Illus. 176).

Illus. 176. Hole for hourglass projection.

3. Scribe a circle on the face of the disc with the point of the beading and parting tool. You can use this line as a center for the spacers and as a guide to prevent overcutting the edge moulding (Illus. 177). Mould the edge and finish completely. It may be necessary to re-establish the spacer middle line if it gets removed by the abrasives, but be careful to leave a neat finish because it will remain in the final design.

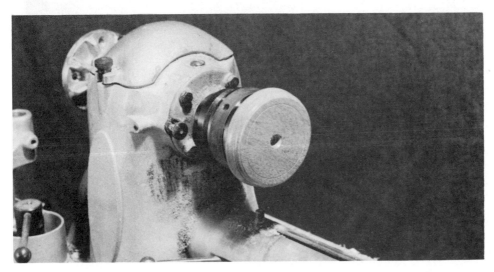

Illus. 177. Circular mark for spacer middle line.

4. To mark the centers for the spacers, set a pair of compasses to a radius of the scribed line and then carefully set six marks around the circle (Illus. 178).

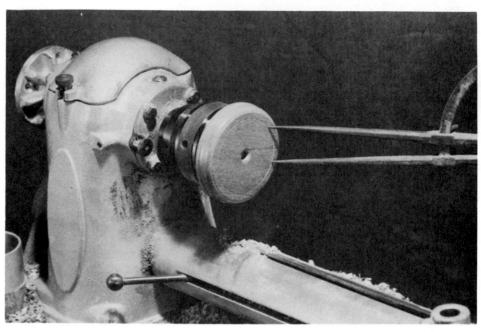

Illus. 178. Scribe marks for spacers.

5. With a ¼″ bit, drill three of the marks at 12, 4, and 8 o'clock to a depth of ⅜″ (Illus. 179). Repeat this procedure for the second disc, making sure that the ring is scribed exactly in the same place to align the spacers correctly.

Illus. 179. Drill the holes.

6. Remove the discs and place the hourglass between them to measure the distance from face to face. This will establish the exact spacer height, to which you should add 1″ for the spigots. Place the first blank between centers and turn the spacer to your own design, remembering to turn a spigot at each end. Size the spigot to fit the holes in the discs; then completely finish according to Method 1. Make two more spacers to the same design (Illus. 180). Now glue and assemble the piece.

Illus. 180. Make three spacers.

30
INLAID JEWELRY BOX

Illus. 181.

WOOD

Rough-sawn beech, sycamore, cherry, or anything else that is suitable
4″ × 4″ length, optional
Inlaid banding of your choice

LATHE ACCESSORIES

Screw chuck with plywood-backed washer
Revolving center

	Saw-toothed machine center bit, large
OTHER TOOLS	Skew chisel, 1¼″
	Straight-across chisel, 1¼″
	Beading and parting tool, ⅜″
	Parting tool, conventional or fluted
	Roughing gouge, ¾″ or larger
	Scrapers—1″ scraper for inside box lid and body, and narrow homemade scraper for inlay
FINISHING	Method 1
DIFFICULTY	Grade C

1. Fix the workpiece to the screw chuck, supporting it with the revolving center, and rough down to a cylinder with the roughing gouge. Mark the outer circumference of the lid lip, and remove the central waste to a depth of ⅜″ using a scraper (Illus. 182).

Illus. 182. Remove waste from lid.

2. Completely finish the interior of the lid, and then mark its total length with a pencil, while also delineating the base of the box. Part off with the fluted parting tool (Illus. 183); then tidy the end grain with the skew, using light cuts to avoid disturbing the workpiece.

Illus. 183. Part off lid.

3. Mark the cylinder ⅜″ from the end and score a line with the beading and parting tool. Reduce the right-hand end to a diameter equal to the diameter of the lid opening (Illus. 184). You can try the lid on the box for a trial fit, but do not push the lid onto the revolving work because this will cause the lip to become eroded and oversized very quickly.

Illus. 184. Form spigot.

4. Using the large bit, remove the maximum amount of waste from the center of the box (Illus. 185). Frequently withdraw the bit for

cooling and removal of shavings. When the waste has been removed, arrange an adjustable lamp to shine into the hole.

Illus. 185. Remove waste from box.

5. Enlarge the interior of the box and then finish completely using Method 1 on page 213 or any method you prefer (Illus. 186). The interior shape is arbitrary, although the sides should be parallel.

Illus. 186. Finish interior.

6. Fit the lid, looking for the best grain match, and then dome the lid by making light cuts with the skew (Illus. 187). A quick pass with the roughing gouge will ensure a perfect match of the base and lid, but keep a light touch.

Illus. 187. Dome lid.

7. Carefully mark the base for the inlay grooves (Illus. 188). The lip on the lid, produced by the beading and parting tool, makes it easier to remove the lid.

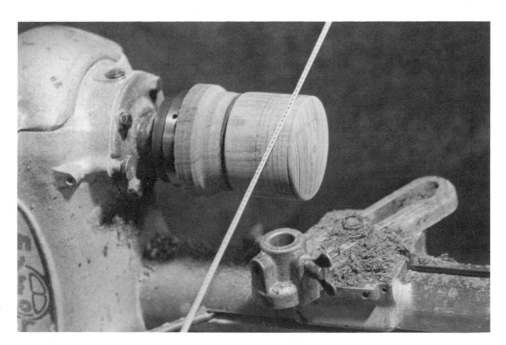

Illus. 188. Mark box for inlay.

8. Reduce the grooves with a small scraper, checking both the width and depth of the cut against the inlay strip (Illus. 189). The groove should be slightly shallower than the thickness of the strip to allow for blending in.

Illus. 189. Small scraper forms groove.

9. Apply a polyvinyl acetate (PVA) glue to the grooves and feed in the inlay before cutting it to size. Press it home with a block of wood, and trim to size as the two ends meet, thereby ensuring an accurate joint (Illus. 190). The cut can be diagonal or straight, whichever blends best into the inlay design. Make light passes with the roughing gouge to blend in the inlay and the sides of the box; then glasspaper and finish according to Method 1 or a method you may prefer.

Illus. 190. Press home inlay with wood block.

31
INLAID VANITY MIRROR

Illus. 191.

WOOD	Any suitable disc blank 5″ in diameter and ¾″ thick Handle: 1″ × 1″ × 6″ Inlay strip
OTHER MATERIALS	Mirror, 3½″ in diameter
LATHE ACCESSORIES	Combination chuck or coil chuck with dovetail fitting Pillar drill Drill bit, ⅜″ Four-pronged driving center Revolving center
OTHER TOOLS	Superflute bowl gouge

Straight-across scraper
Narrow parting tool

FINISHING   Method 1 or 4

DIFFICULTY   Grade C

1. You should make the back first. Select the screw-chuck assembly for the combination chuck, and mount the blank with its flattest surface against the chuck face. True the edge of the circle and face off the surface of the disc with the Superflute gouge (Illus. 192).

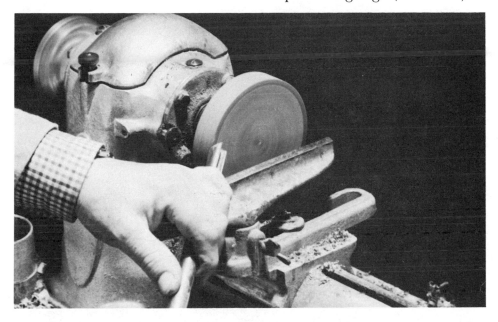

Illus. 192. True disc.

2. Now you should make two rabbets, one for the mirror and the other for the backing hardboard (Illus. 193). Mark a ring on the disc face to accept the mirror, but include a small tolerance to allow a slack fit for wood expansion. Remove the waste to a depth of ¼″, which is the same depth as the mirror thickness plus the hardboard backing. Offer the mirror, checking for a slack fit; then draw a line inside the edge of the rabbet, using the back of the mirror to set the depth of the line. This will establish the depth of the second rabbet. Mark a line ¼″ outside the mirror rabbet and then remove the waste down to the mirror-depth pencil line.

To provide a clean finish when cutting through from the reverse face (after reversing the disc on the chuck), scribe a line with the point of the parting tool that is 3⅛″ in diameter. This will cleanly cut the fibres and minimize breakout when you break through later.

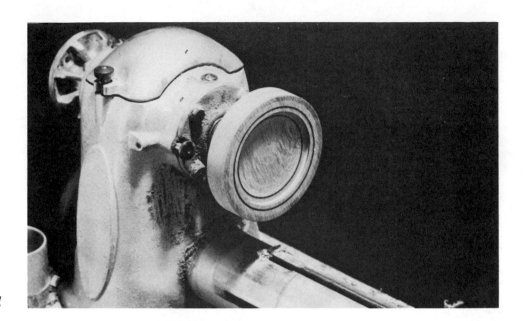

3. Remove the disc, select the dovetail assembly of the chuck, and fit the dovetail into the rabbet (Illus. 194). Turn the outside diameter to 4½″ and face the surface of the disc to a thickness of ⅝″. Mark a ring that is 3⅛″ in diameter on the face of the disc to correspond with the mark on the other side, and then remove the central waste with the parting tool. Note that the disc doesn't have a backing piece, so take care when breaking through to avoid damaging the chuck. When the tool is almost through the disc, you will hear a distinct change in the sound that is made.

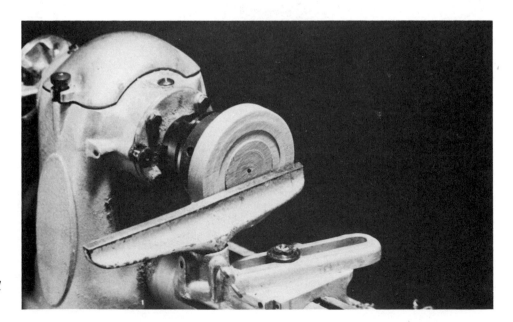

Illus. 194. Disc reversed onto dovetail.

4. Now remove the waste. Note the dovetail assembly of the chuck (Illus. 195).

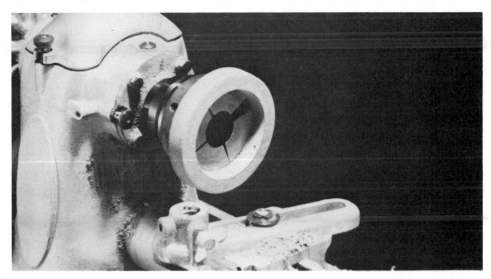

Illus. 195. Central waste removed.

5. Dish the rim of the frame with the Superflute gouge and shape to your own design. Mark two lines on the outer rim to accept the inlay and then form a rabbet with a narrow scraper. Constantly check the inlay strip against the rabbet for a tight fit. Now brush glue into the rabbet and feed in the inlay, using the back of an old toothbrush to press it home (Illus. 196). Do not cut the inlay until it is fully settled in the rabbet; then cut at the overlap. Finish with abrasives to blend in the inlay; the heat built up by the friction will cause the glue to set more quickly. Completely finish according to Method 1 on page 213, Method 4 on page 214, or to your own preference, and then set aside.

Illus. 196. Press the inlay home.

6. Fix the handle blank between centers and turn to your own design, leaving a spigot ⅞″ long and ⅜″ in diameter to fit into the mirror head (Illus. 197). With the pillar drill, drill the hole in the mirror rim for the handle, using the joint in the inlay as a center. When you insert the handle, the joint will be hidden.

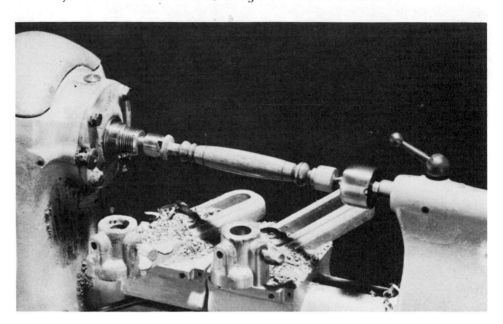

Illus. 197. Turn handle.

32
RING TREE

Illus. 198.

WOOD

Base: disc blank, 3½″ × 1″
Central column: ¾″ × ¾″ ×
  3″
Arms: ½″ × ½″ × 3¼″

LATHE ACCESSORIES

Screw chuck
Revolving center
Small driving center
Pillar drill

OTHER TOOLS

Superflute bowl gouge
Roughing gouge

Skew chisel, 1¼″
Spindle gouge
Beading and parting tool

FINISHING　　　　　　　Method 1

DIFFICULTY　　　　　　Grade C

1. You need to make the base first (Illus. 199). Find the center of the disc and drill a hole right through to accept the screw of the screw chuck. Fix the disc to the screw chuck, and face the front surface with the Superflute gouge. A slightly dished finish is desirable because this face will form the base when you reverse the work. True the edge and then finish the face with abrasives.

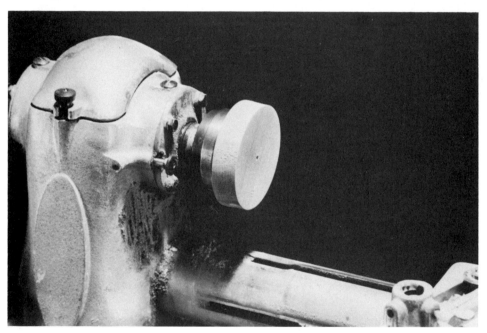

Illus. 199. Make the base first.

2. Reverse the blank on the screw chuck and true the edge. Mould the edge to your own design and, with a small gouge, form a central base frame, dishing the central circle around the hole to provide a firm base for the central column (Illus. 200). Ideally, the middle of the base frame should finish at a ⅝″ diameter. Finish completely, following Method 1 on page 213 or another method you may prefer. With a ⅜″ drill bit, enlarge the spigot hole to a diameter of ⅜″ and a depth of *no more than* ⅛″ to avoid the screw of the chuck. This will provide a start for the pillar drill, which you will use later to drill the hole for the central column.

3. Fix the central column blank between centers and rough down to the largest diameter (Illus. 201). Turn a spigot ⅜″ in diameter and ½″ long, forming a shoulder above the spigot that is ⅝″ in diameter to exactly cover the top of the base frame.

Illus. 201. The central column.

4. Shape the central column, finishing the cylinder on the right-hand side at a diameter of ⅝″ to ensure that it will rest horizontally in the V-block during drilling (Illus. 202). The ring shown in Illus. 201

is incorporated into the design to provide a middle line for drilling the hole for the arms.

5. Fix the arm blank between centers and rough down to the largest diameter (Illus. 203). Mark a small waste area of ¼″ at each end to provide holding pips, and scribe a line at the middle of the cylinder. Measure and scribe a line ¼″ on either side of the middle mark, and then reduce the waste in between to form a spigot to enter the central column.

Illus. 203. The arm blank.

6. Mark the middle line on the central spigot again to provide a guide for sawing the piece in two to form the two arms (Illus. 204). Finish completely according to Method 1 or another method you may prefer, but leave the spigot free of polish to facilitate gluing. Part off and then saw into two pieces. Assemble the base and central column; then glue in the arms.

Illus. 204. Mark middle for sawing.

33
GOBLET WITH LID

Illus. 205.

WOOD   Anything suitable
                             3″ × 3″ × 10½″

LATHE ACCESSORIES   Spigot chuck
                             Screw chuck
                             Jacob's chuck
                             Large saw-toothed machine
                                center bit
                             Plug with cloth

OTHER TOOLS   Roughing gouge

Beading and parting tool
Fluted parting tool
Roundnose scraper
Skew chisel, 1¼"
Spindle gouge
Vernier calipers

FINISHING   Method 4

DIFFICULTY   Grade C

1. Place the workpiece between the centers and reduce it to a cylinder, forming a suitable spigot for your chuck. Insert the spigot into the chuck and true the cylinder, making sure the end farthest from the chuck is centered to avoid vibration (Illus. 206). Correct balance at this point is very important. Square the end grain with the skew.

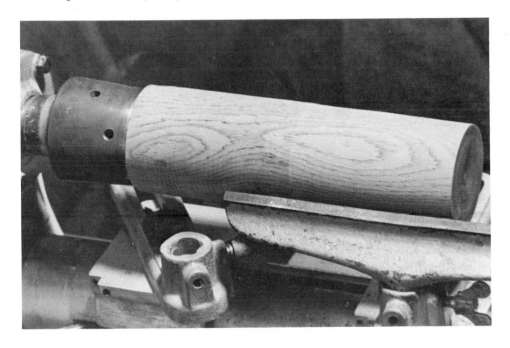

Illus. 206. The cylinder centered in the spigot chuck.

2. Drill through the center to a depth of approximately 1⅜". Mark the outer diameter in pencil. Remove the waste with the roundnose scraper, following the profile in Illus. 207. To avoid tearing the grain, work the scraper from the bottom of the hole to the top, undercutting the sides. At this stage, it's helpful to use a light shining inside the hollow.

When the tool work is complete, glass-paper to a finish. Be very careful not to build up too much friction-generated heat, which will crack the end grain. At this stage, do not finish beyond glass-papering.

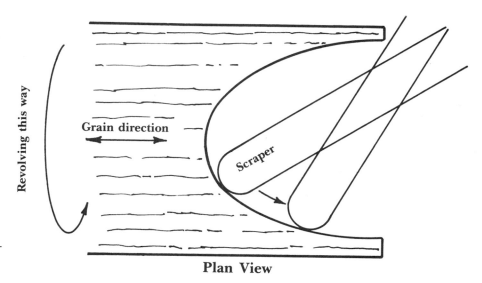

Revolving this way

Grain direction

Scraper

Plan View

Illus. 207. Internal profile.

3. Add ⅜″ to the internal depth and place a pencil mark on the cylinder as a rough guide. Mark the other dimensions of the goblet according to your personal preference. As a guide, the dimensions shown in Illus. 208 are 1¾″ (top to first mark), 3⅛″ (stem), and ⅞″ (base). Scribe with the beading and parting tool.

Illus. 208. Mark dimensions of goblet on cylinder.

4. Insert a large wooden plug into the hole to allow the reduction of a fine stem with minimal vibration (Illus. 209). (Chapter 44 contains instructions on making your own plug.) With the beading and parting tool, initially reduce the stem to a 1½″ diameter.

5. Remove the plug and shape the outside of the bowl with the spindle gouge, constantly checking the wall thickness with your fingers (Illus. 210). Where the shaping is complete, glass-paper to a finish.

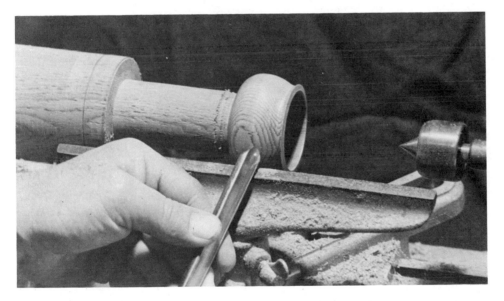

Illus. 210. Carefully shape outside of bowl.

6. Reinsert the plug and reduce the base diameter, which is usually made smaller than the bowl diameter for aesthetic reasons (Illus. 211). Using the fluted parting tool, reduce the spindle below the base. Enlarge this groove with the beading and parting tool to allow the skew access so that it can clean the end grain at the edge of the base. This will later form a flat surface for a baize ring.

Illus. 211. Reinsert the plug to work the base and stem.

7. Shape the stem, working from the base of the bowl to the base of the stem. The distance from the base of the bowl to the base of the stem has now been reduced by waste removal to 1½". Note the slight curve in the profile of the stem; a straight line has been deliberately avoided (Illus. 212). Glass-paper to a finish.

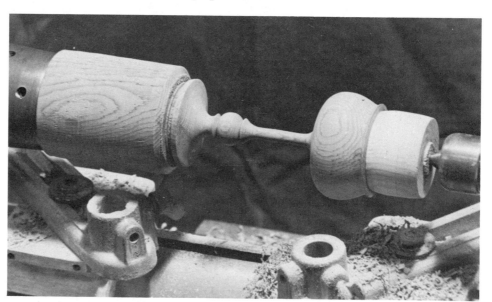

Illus. 212. The completed stem and base.

8. To part the goblet, cut into a diameter of ³⁄₁₆" with the fluted parting tool. Undercut the base to make sure that it will stand firm and then remove the plug. Place your fingers under the stem, allowing it to revolve in your hand, and ease it away from the handrest while completing the parting cut (Illus. 213). Set the goblet aside.

9. Make the lid from the remaining wood after first making one or two light passes with the roughing gouge to make sure that it is correctly centered in the chuck. Square off the end grain with the skew, and measure the internal diameter of the goblet bowl with the vernier calipers. Scribe the cylinder ⅛″ from the end, and reduce it with the beading and parting tool to the correct diameter. Constantly check the diameter and, when it's correct, undercut the rim to match the goblet lip and remove the center with a gouge, leaving a dished hollow (Illus. 214).

Illus. 214. Completed base of lid.

10. Determine the height of the lid; then mark and scribe the cylinder. Shape the top of the lid with a small spindle gouge and glass paper (Illus. 215). Part with the skew, leaving a finished surface where the skew cuts. Make a hole in the top of the lid with a bradawl to accept a screw eye for holding and hanging while applying the plastic finish. (The hole will also accept the knob after it's enlarged with a suitable drill bit.)

Illus. 215. Forming the lid.

11. Reduce the remaining waste to the outer diameter of the knob, and then shape using a small spindle gouge (Illus. 216). As an alternative, you can make the knob on a screw chuck.

Illus. 216. Waste reduced for knob.

12. Leave a small spigot that is ¼″ in diameter to fit into the lid and then part off (Illus. 217). Make a small hole in the spigot to accept a screw eye. Apply plastic finish to the goblet, lid, and knob according to Method 4 on page 214 or another method you may prefer; then hang them up to dry. Assemble when finished.

Illus. 217. The finished knob and spigot.

34
CANDLESTICK

Illus. 218.

WOOD

Any straight-grained hardwood
2½″ × 2½″ × 9″
You can vary the length to suit
  your own candle.

LATHE ACCESSORIES

Screw chuck
Revolving center
Plug

OTHER TOOLS

Roughing gouge
Beading and parting tool

Spindle gouge
Skew chisel, 1¼″
Drill bit for candle

FINISHING   Method 1

DIFFICULTY   Grade C

1. Using the revolving center to steady it, place the workpiece on the screw chuck and turn down to the largest diameter. Scribe the cylinder for the top and base design (Illus. 219). Tidy the end grain with the skew, leaving a pip over the revolving center.

Illus. 219. Mark the cylinder with your own design.

2. Drill out the hole for the candle to a depth of ⅞″ (Illus. 220).

Illus. 220. Drilling the candle hole.

3. Insert the plug (see Chapter 44 if you want to make your own). Using the roughing gouge, rough down to the basic shape (Illus. 221). Delineate the base at this stage.

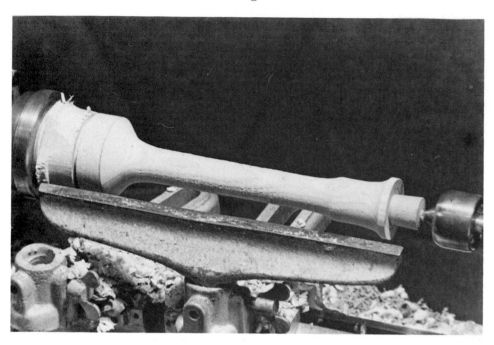

Illus. 221. Rough down to the basic pattern.

4. Using the spindle gouge, shape the bowl and the top half of the stem (Illus. 222). Glass-paper at this stage because the fragile stem will prevent further work on the bowl.

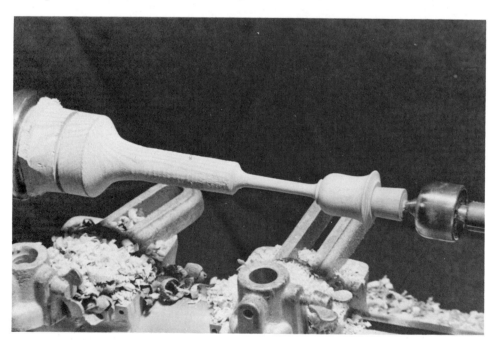

Illus. 222. Shape the bowl and half the stem.

5. Shape the bottom half of the stem and glass-paper to a finish. Polish and part off. For finishing instructions, see Method 1 on page 213.

Note the distinct break in design between the stem and base, the stem and bowl, and the turned lip on the base (Illus. 223). These design features appear in many situations in wood turning and contribute towards a professional finish.

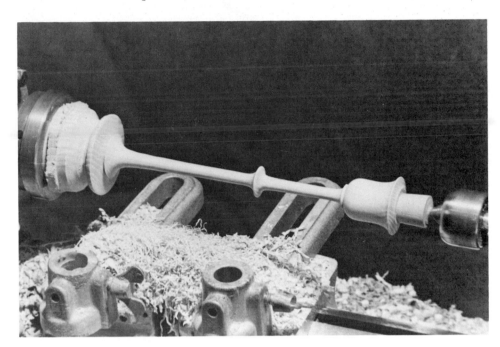

Illus. 223. The completed piece.

35
NUTMEG GRINDER

Illus. 224.

WOOD	Yew, ash, mahogany, or anything else that is suitable 4⅛″ × 2″ × 2″
OTHER MATERIALS	Grinder mechanism
LATHE ACCESSORIES	Four-pronged driving center Revolving center Saw-toothed machine center bit, 1″ Long series drill bit, ¼″ Plug
OTHER TOOLS	Roughing gouge Skew chisel, 1¼″ Beading and parting tool

Spindle gouge
Fluted parting tool

FINISHING   Method 3 or 4

DIFFICULTY   Grade C

1. The grinder mechanism that will be inserted inside the turned body is shown in Illus. 225.

Illus. 225. The grinder mechanism.

2. Predrill the blank to accept the mechanism and the nutmeg according to the dimensions of your mechanism and the instructions that came with it. The measurements in this example are only intended as a guide; you should take your own measurements from the apparatus you are using. Find the middle of the blank and drill a hole that is 1″ in diameter and 3⁷⁄₁₆″ deep to provide a tunnel for the pronged gripper and the nutmeg. Using the middle as a guide, drill through the remainder of the blank with a ¼″ bit for the shank (Illus. 226).

3. Mount the blank in the lathe, using the plug in the large hole and the revolving center in the smaller hole (Illus. 227). (For instructions on making your own plug, turn to Chapter 44.) Turn down to a cylinder and then square the end grain at the plug end using the skew chisel.

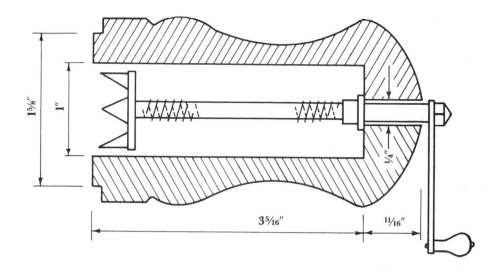

Illus. 226. Note that spring is compressed before nutmeg is inserted.

Illus. 227. Plug in position.

4. At the left-hand side, mark the cylinder ¹⁄₁₆″ from the end (which is the same as the internal depth of the base ring), scribe with the beading and parting tool, and reduce to a diameter of 1¹¹⁄₁₆″ so that the ring can slip over the small protruding spigot. Slightly round the shoulder of the cylinder (Illus. 228).

5. Measure the shank of the grinder from the pronged gripper to the handle, directly below the retaining nut (in this example, it's 3¾″). Transfer this measurement to the cylinder, measuring from

the extreme base on the left to the top of the right-hand side, next to the revolving center. Scribe and then make a partial parting cut, remembering not to cut too deep since the center has been drilled; leave a holding pip over the revolving center. Shape the cylinder, dome the top with the skew chisel, and finish according to Method 3 or 4 on page 214 or to another method you may prefer. Remove and assemble (Illus. 229).

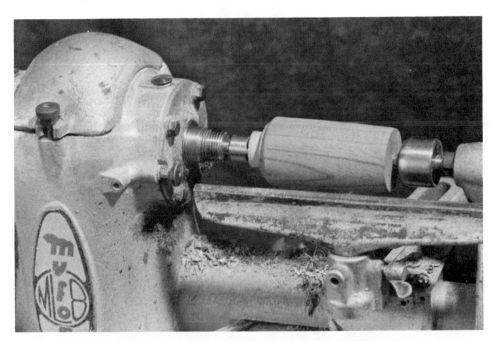

Illus. 228. Form shoulder for base ring.

Illus. 229. Ready for polishing and assembly.

36
SALT GRINDER

Illus. 230.

WOOD

You can use any exotic hardwood, but coccoloba or English yew are especially recommended.

Two pieces, 2½″ × 2½″ × 2⅛

OTHER MATERIALS

Grinder mechanism and glass body

LATHE ACCESSORIES

Screw chuck
Revolving center

	Jacob's chuck
	Large saw-toothed machine center bit
	Two plugs
OTHER TOOLS	Roughing gouge
	Skew chisel, 1¼″
	Spindle gouge
	Beading and parting tool
	Fluted parting tool
	Straight-across scraper
FINISHING	Method 1 or 4
DIFFICULTY	Grade C

1. You need to make the top first. Fix the blank on the screw chuck and, using the revolving center to steady it, rough down to the largest diameter. Square the end grain with the skew, slightly undercutting the end of the cylinder. Drill a hole ½″ deep and then enlarge it to 1³⁄₁₆″ in diameter to accept the top of the glass body (Illus. 231).

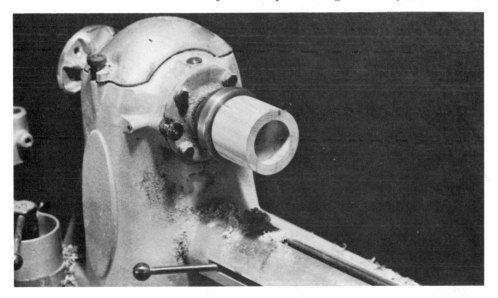

Illus. 231. Top drilled to accept glass.

2. Remove the workpiece from the screw chuck. Using the hole left by the screw chuck as a guide, drill a hole right through the middle for the spindle of the mechanism. This hole should be about ¼″ in diameter. Select a suitable plug for the larger hole and chuck again with the revolving center in the smaller hole (Illus. 232). (To make your own plug, follow the instructions in Chapter 44.)

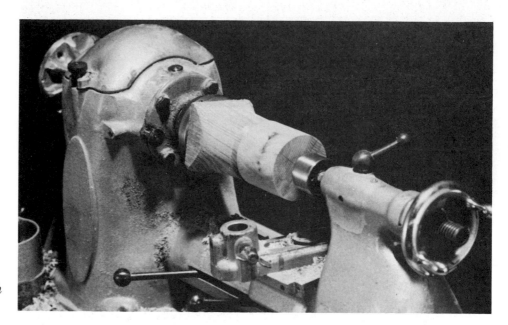

Illus. 232. Rechuck with large plug.

3. Turn the top knob according to your own design and to suit your mechanism (Illus. 233). In this example, the cylinder was reduced to a length of 2″ with a fluted parting tool and to a diameter of 2½″ with a roughing gouge. Finish completely according to Method 1 on page 213, Method 4 on page 214, or another method you may prefer; then part off.

Illus. 233. Turn to your own design.

4. Fix the base blank to the screw chuck and rough down to the largest diameter; square the end grain with the skew, slightly under-cutting as before. Drill a 1½″-diameter hole ³⁄₁₆″ deep for the grinder

mechanism, as well as another hole to accept the
when you reverse the piece (Illus. 234).

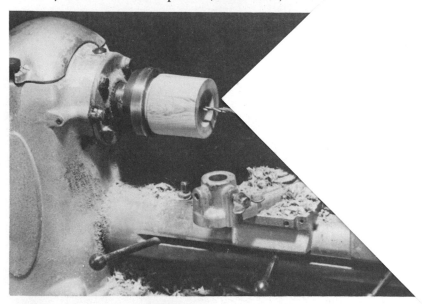

5. Reverse the base on the chuck and reduce the cylinder to a .
of 2". Take care while working on the base from this point on
cause the screw of the chuck is only holding at its extremity. Drill ou.
the waste to a diameter of 1³⁄₁₆" and a depth of ½" to accept the glass
(Illus. 235). If you buy a separate rubber expansion ring for the base
section, you need to allow for it when removing the waste. Start a 1"-
diameter hole on the lathe for the mechanism; move the workpiece
to the pillar drill and, using this center as a guide, drill right
through.

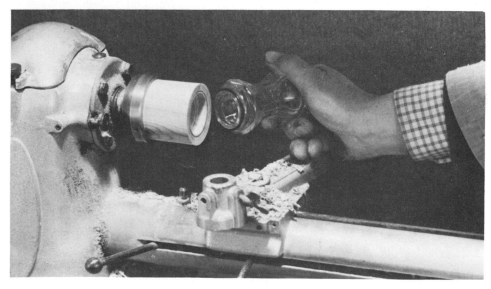

Illus. 235. Check the fit.

his is a good time to make a trial assembly of all the parts, taking
of any necessary adjustments. Rechuck the base using two
gs, noting the top and bottom of the base, and then turn down to
ur design (Illus. 236). Finish completely according to Method 1 on
page 213, Method 4 on page 214, or to another method you may
prefer; then remove and assemble.

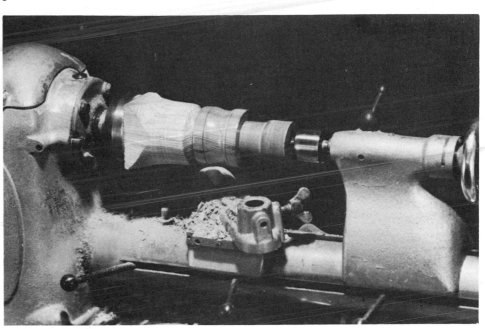

236. Turn the

37
PEPPER GRINDER

Illus. 237.

WOOD

Any straight-grained hardwood
2¼″ × 2¼″ × 9″ body
  for a 1″ mechanism,
  or 2¼″ × 2¼″ × 7″ body
with separate 2¼″ × 2¼″ ×
2″ lid

OTHER MATERIALS   Grinder mechanism

LATHE ACCESSORIES   Four-pronged driving center
Revolving center
Screw chuck

	Jacob's chuck and drill bits to suit mechanism
	Two suitable plugs
OTHER TOOLS	Roughing gouge
	Skew chisel, 1¼″
	Spindle gouge
	Beading and parting tool
FINISHING	Method 4
DIFFICULTY	Grade C

1. Place the blank on the screw chuck and drill a hole to accommodate the bottom bracket of the mechanism. In this example, the hole is ⁵⁄₁₆″ deep, allowing for a ¹⁄₁₀″ trim of end grain (Illus. 238).

Illus. 238. Drill hole for bottom bracket.

2. Drill another hole that is 1″ in diameter and ³⁄₈″ deep below the floor of the first hole (Illus. 239). This hole is part of the peppercorn chamber; you will drill into it from the other side when you reverse the work. Drilling from this end first ensures that the grinder mechanism will be lined up with the bottom bracket.

Reverse the workpiece, filling the bottom hole with a suitable plug. (To make your own plug, follow the instructions in Chapter 44.) Drill a 1¼″-diameter hole for the lid that is ³⁄₈″ deep. Drill another hole 1″ in diameter right through the piece, using the first hole as a center. This hole will break into the 1″-diameter hole drilled in the base.

Since any slight misalignment will be concealed in the grinder body, it will not be critical.

When you've completed the drilling, plug both ends and fix between centers (Illus. 240).

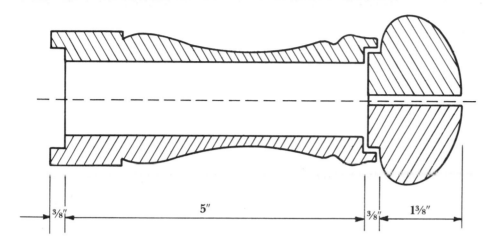

3/8"   5"   3/8"   1 3/8"

Illus. 239. Cross section of pepper mill.

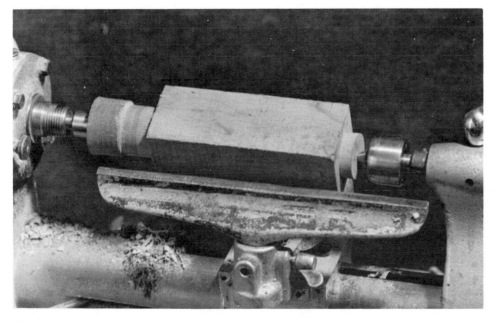

Illus. 240. Both ends plugged.

3. Rough down the work to the largest diameter and then square the end grain on both ends with the skew (Illus. 241).

4. Remove the workpiece from the lathe and select a blank for the lid. First mark the centers at both ends and drive a four-pronged center into the work; then remove it and drill a hole for the central spindle, which is usually ¼" in diameter. Fix between centers (Illus. 242).

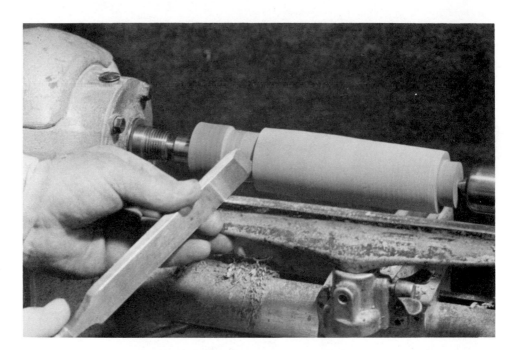

Illus. 241. Square end grain with skew.

Illus. 242. The lid blank after drilling.

5. Rough down the work to the largest diameter and then scribe a line 1/10″ from the right-hand end. With the beading and parting tool, reduce it to slightly less than 1¼″ for a slack fit and to allow for subsequent wood movement. This lip will fit the 1¼″-diameter hole previously drilled in the body (Illus. 243).

6. Fit the lid into the body and then plug the left-hand end, fixing the entire assembly between centers. True the cylinder with the roughing gouge and match in the lid. Shape the body and lid to your own design (Illus. 244).

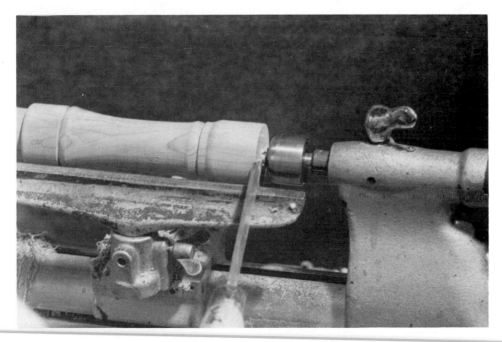

Illus. 244. Rough out to your own design.

7. Finish the workpiece completely according to Method 4 on page 214 or to another method you may prefer; then remove it and assemble the mechanism (Illus. 245).

Illus. 245. The finished mill.

8. If you prefer to turn the body and lid separately, finish the lid completely and add it to the body at the assembly stage (Illus. 246).

Illus. 246. Lid turned separately.

38
GAVEL AND BLOCK

Illus. 247.

WOOD

Handle: 1¼″ × 1¼″ × 9″ and
   1¼″ × 1¼″ × 2½″
Head: 2¼″ × 2¼″ × 5″
Block: 4¾″ (diameter) × 1½″
   (thickness)
Block insert: 2½″ × 2½″ × ¾″

THE ACCESSORIES

Four-pronged driving center
Revolving center
Screw chuck

OLS

Roughing gouge
Skew chisel, 1¼″
Spindle gouge
Beading and parting tool
Small scraper

FINISHING DIFFICULTY

Method 1 or 4

Grade C

1. Fix the handle blank between centers and turn to your own design (Illus. 248). Note the spigot at the left-hand end, which will fit into the head. Finish completely, but do not remove the holding pips at this stage or apply finish to the spigot. This will be trimmed later to fit into the gavel head. Remove the workpiece from the lathe and set it carefully aside.

Illus. 248. Turn handle to own design.

2. Insert the gavel head blank between centers and rough down to the largest diameter, cutting a holding pip at each side. Make sure that the pip at the driving center has enough clearance for you to dome the head with the skew chisel. Measure and scribe a line exactly in the middle to provide a guide for drilling (Illus. 249).

3. Remove the workpiece and then drill a hole to the diameter of the handle spigot right through the head (Illus. 250). Be careful not to split the wood at the drill-exit point. Replace the workpiece betwee[n] centers and completely finish according to Method 1 on page 2[1], Method 4 on page 214, or to your own design. Part off.

4. Fix the remaining handle blank between centers and tu[rn] match the handle design. This is a false end to the handle [...]

own spigot, giving the appearance that the handle passes completely through the head when assembled (Illus. 251). Finish, except for the spigot, and measure the depth of the hole in the gavel head. Part the spigot so that it will penetrate to half this depth. Replace the main handle section between centers, and then part off at the spigot.

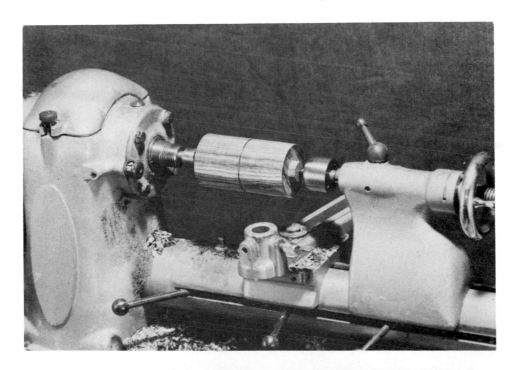

Illus. 249. Scribe middle line.

Illus. 250. Hole drilled completely through.

Illus. 251. The false handle end.

5. Assemble the three components (Illus. 252) and then glue with epoxy cement.

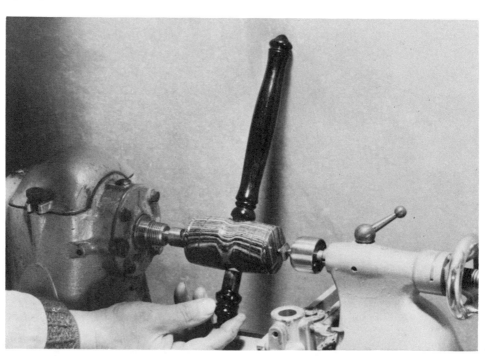

Illus. 252. The three components.

6. Fix the block blank onto the screw chuck and, using the revolving center to steady it, rough down to the largest diameter (Illus. 253). Dome the end grain with a spindle gouge to provide a striking

surface on the gavel. Finish according to Method 1 on page 213, Method 4 on page 214, or another method you may prefer; then part off at a thickness of ½″.

Illus. 253. Block insert.

7. Drill a hole right through the block-base blank to accept the screw of the screw chuck. Fix the blank onto the chuck and then true the edge and face. Reverse the blank and open out the hole to accept the block insert with a scraper. Shape the edge, noting the coves at the midway point and top lip (Illus. 254).

Illus. 254. Prepared block base.

8. Finish the base according to Method 1 or 4 or another method you may prefer; then glue in the block (Illus. 255).

Illus. 255. Glue in the block.

39
THREE-LEGGED SWISS MILKING STOOL

Illus. 256.

WOOD

Seat: Use a seasoned disc
blank, 12″ × 3″ thick. If you
are preparing a blank to set
aside for seasoning, it will
require a flat rim ½″ in

diameter with the middle dished to a depth of ⅝″. Ash is ideal for the project.

Legs: Use three pieces, 2″ × 2″ × 17″.

LATHE ACCESSORIES Use a faceplate, 6″ in diameter with three holes drilled at 12, 4, and 8 o'clock that are 2⅝″ from the center. The holes leave accurate marks for drilling the leg holes.

OTHER TOOLS Superflute bowl gouge
Pillar drill
1″ saw-toothed machine center bit
Beading and parting tool

FINISHING Method 2

DIFFICULTY Grade C

1. Select a seasoned disc blank for the seat (Illus. 257), plane the bottom, and finish with abrasives. Fit it to the faceplate with three screws.

Illus. 257. The seasoned seat blank.

2. With the Superflute gouge, turn the outside to the finished profile. Note the twist in the seat face, which has occurred during seasoning (Illus. 258).

Illus. 258. The outside profile.

3. Dish the seat of the stool to a depth of ½″, leaving ½″ flat on the rim (Illus. 259). Finish the inside and outside with abrasives.

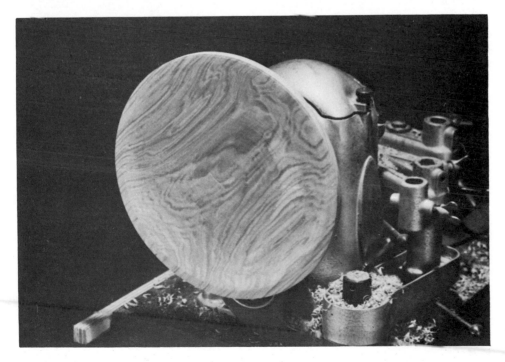

Illus. 259. Dish middle of seat, leaving flat rim.

4. With the beading and parting tool, cut a fine bead on the lip of the seat to give a professional finish to the design (Illus. 260).

Illus. 260. The bead on the lip.

5. Fix the blank for the first leg between centers and turn to your own design. The example, shown in Illus. 261, follows basic design principles with its long, flowing lines, and is a perfect match for the stool seat. The spigot at the left-hand end (the top) should finish at a diameter 1/16″ larger than the hole diameter, which is drilled in the base of the seat to accept the leg. After turning the spigot to size, finish the leg completely according to Method 2 on page 213 or another method you may prefer and then apply Danish oil.

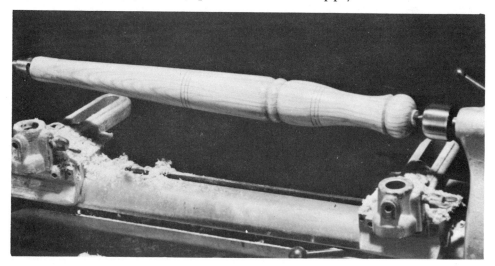

Illus. 261. Note flowing lines of the design.

6. Drill three holes in the seat base on the pillar drill, using the screw holes from the chuck as centers (Illus. 262).

Illus. 262. Drill the base.

7. To fit a leg to the seat, heat the spigot over a slow fire for ½ hour, being careful not to burn it. You can then hammer the leg home with a mallet when enough shrinkage has taken place; the leg will expand to a tight fit as the wood reabsorbs moisture from the air. If you use this traditional method of assembly, glue is not required to hold the legs in place. Repeat this process for the two other legs.

40 POMANDER

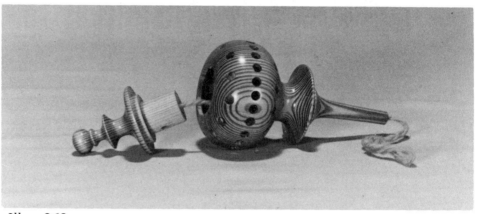

Illus. 263.

WOOD   Any hardwood or softwood
                            3½″ × 3½″ × 9″

OTHER MATERIALS   Herbs

LATHE ACCESSORIES   Spigot chuck
                            Revolving center
                            Saw-toothed machine center
                               bit, 1⅜″
                            Jacob's chuck

OTHER TOOLS   Roughing gouge
                            Skew chisel, 1¼″
                            Beading and parting tool
                            Spindle gouge
                            Drill with ¼″ bit for holes in
                               pomander and ⅛″ bit for
                               spigot
                            Roundnose scraper

FINISHING   Method 1 or 4

DIFFICULTY   Grade C

1. You should make the base first. Insert the blank into the spigot chuck and rough down to the largest diameter. Turn the base to the bulbous shape, and drill through the middle with the 1⅜" bit (Illus. 264). Hollow out the center with a scraper so that the wall thickness of the hole follows the profile of the outside. This is important because the wall thickness will be visible through the holes.

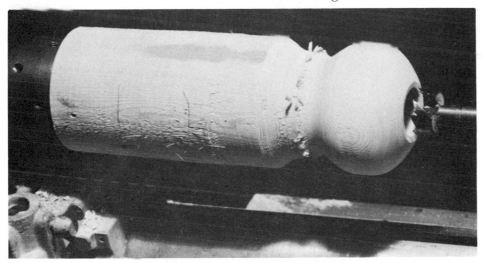

Illus. 264. Drill through the base.

2. Insert a plug into the hole in the base and turn the top (Illus. 265). Be careful to keep the lines of the design free and flowing. Glasspaper and finish according to Method 1 on page 213, Method 4 on page 214, or another method you may prefer.

Illus. 265. The plug in position.

3. Use a drill mounted on the lathe bed to make the three lines of holes, which allow the aroma to escape. A homemade apparatus is shown in Illus. 266.

Illus. 266. Drill the holes.

4. An enlargement of the drilling operation is shown in Illus. 267. (To prevent the herbs from leaking through the holes, you will need to put them in a cheesecloth bag and then place the bag in the hollow.) When the drilling is completed, glass-paper, finish according to Method 1 or 4, and part off.

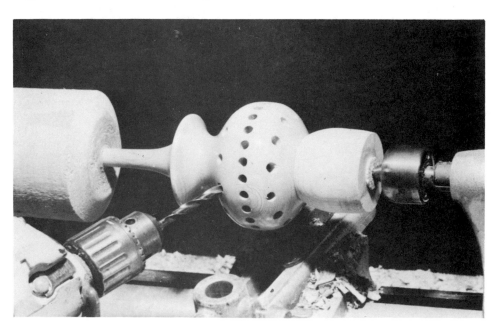

Illus. 267. Drilling detail.

5. Drill a ⅛" hole in the top to accept a string for hanging the pomander (Illus. 268). Pierce the hole right through into the cavity, allowing the string to be fastened in the turned plug at the base. This ensures that the pomander will hang vertically.

Illus. 268. Drill string hole.

6. First, turn the spigot that will accept the string (Illus. 269). Measure the opening in the top and gradually reduce the spigot for a slack fit. Work the coves and beads on the left-hand side; then glass-paper and carefully finish according to Method 1 or 4.

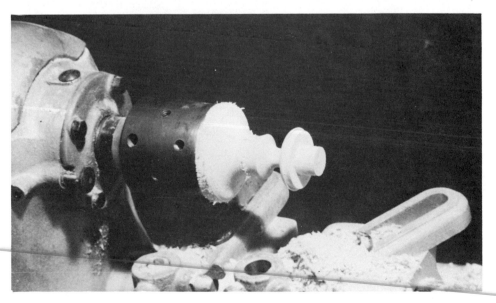

Illus. 269. Turn the spigot first.

7. Drill the ⅛″ hole for the string, using the Jacob's chuck in the tailstock. Drill the ¼″ hole at right angles, using an electric drill, as shown in Illus. 270.

Illus. 270. String-retaining hole.

8. The final check to ensure an accurate fit of the plug is shown in Illus. 271. Remove the top when satisfied and then part off the plug. Feed the string through the top hole and secure it to the plug. Fill the pomander with herbs and then hang it up.

Illus. 271. Check assembly of components.

41
WALKING STICK

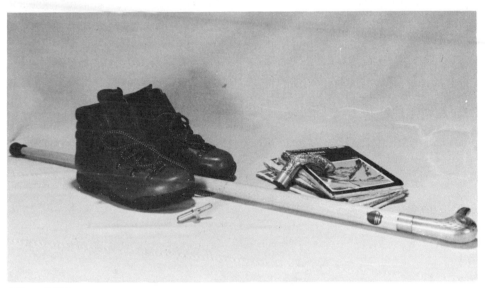

Illus. 272.

WOOD	Use dry, straight-grained hardwood—ash and hickory are ideal. First piece: 1¼″ × 1¼″ × 17″ Second piece: 1¼″ × 1¼″ × 15″
OTHER MATERIALS	Brass fittings
LATHE ACCESSORIES	Four-pronged driving center Revolving center Jacob's chuck Drill bits to suit brass fittings Long tool rest Flat file

OTHER TOOLS	Roughing gouge
	Skew chisel, 1¼″
	Spindle gouge
	Beading and parting tool
	Straight-across chisel
	Fluted parting tool
FINISHING	Method 4
DIFFICULTY	Grade C

1. You make the stick in two parts with a ferrule at the base, a connector at the center, and a ferrule at the top to accept the handle. The bottom is the longer piece and you make it first. Place the Jacob's chuck at the headstock and, using the revolving center for stability, drill a hole in the square stock to accept the (female) threaded-center joint (Illus. 273). Repeat this process for the shorter blank, drilling a hole to accept the other (male) threaded-center joint. Note that this hole is smaller in diameter.

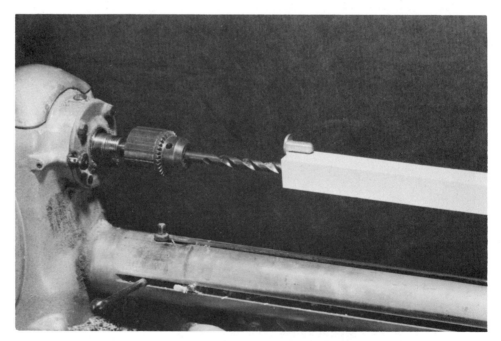

Illus. 273. Drill hole for connector.

2. Refer to Illus. 274 for the alignment of the fittings.

3. Replace the Jacob's chuck with a driving center; fix the 17″ blank between centers, inserting the revolving center into the hole. Turn it down to the largest diameter and then square the end grain at the hole end with the skew, starting the cut with the fluted parting tool to

avoid removing too much waste from the blank. Screw in the brass connector and then place it between centers, allowing the revolving center to run inside the fitting (Illus. 275).

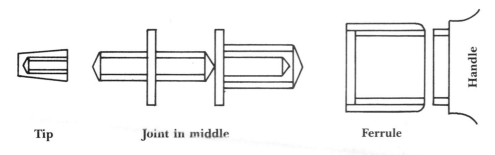

Tip   Joint in middle   Ferrule   Handle

Illus. 274. The brass fittings.

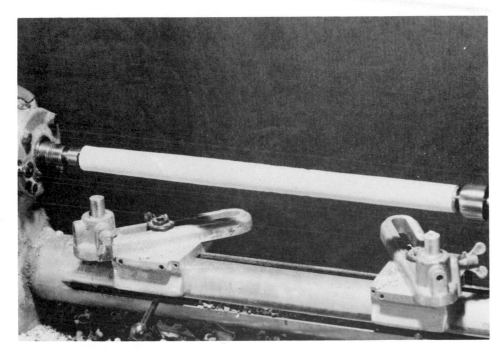

Illus. 275. Revolving center in brass connector.

4. With the roughing gouge, reduce the joint end to the diameter of the brass fitting. Keeping the lathe turning, reduce the diameter of the brass fitting to ⅞″ with a flat file. Taper the stick from the brass fitting towards the headstock, finishing at a diameter that will allow the fitting of the base ferrule. The wood will whip as it becomes thinner, so use your hand to keep it steady (Illus. 276). Plane away any ripples with the straight-across chisel.

5. Carefully size the spigot to fit the ferrule at the base, allowing some tapering (Illus. 277). Finish with abrasives only at this stage. Remove the workpiece from the lathe.

Illus. 276. Support work with hand.

Illus. 277. Note taper at base for ferrule.

6. Mount the second blank in the lathe, with the revolving center in the previously drilled hole. Turn it down to the largest diameter and square the end grain at the hole end as previously described. Fit the smaller connector and then replace the driving center with the Jacob's chuck. Wrap a thin sheet of aluminum around the threads of the connector for protection; then place them between centers, gripping with the chuck as shown in Illus. 278. This fitting will form the center joint and the handle will be fitted to the right-hand end.

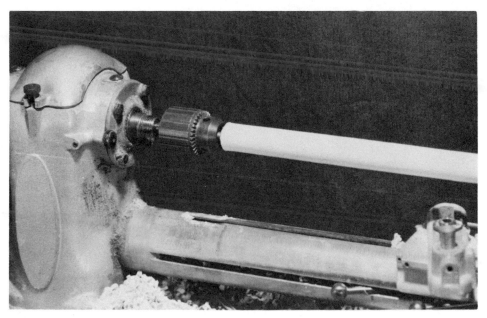

Illus. 278. Chuck grips connector threads.

7. Turn down the connector end to match the diameter of the lower half of the stick at the joint, filing the brass fitting as before. Measure the handle ferrule and then form a spigot at the right-hand end to accept it. Make sure you leave enough clearance inside the ferrule to allow the handle to be fitted to the full depth of its thread without fouling the top of the stick. Taper the stick from right to left as previously described. Assemble the two halves of the stick and fit the handle (Illus. 279); then cover the entire stick, including the brass fittings, with a plastic coat (see Method 4 on page 214).

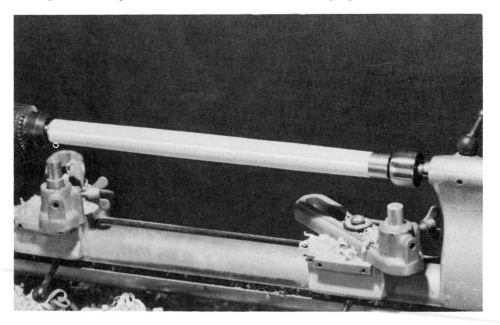

Illus. 279. Handle ferrule in position.

42
TRAVELLER'S CUP

Illus. 280.

WOOD

Collapsible cup: poplar or
  sycamore, 2¼″ × 2¼″ × 4″
Container: a hardwood such as
  yew, 2¼″ × 2¼″ × 6″

LATHE ACCESSORIES

Screw chuck
Revolving center
Saw-toothed machine center
  bits, 1″ and ⅞″
Jacob's chuck
Spigot chuck

OTHER TOOLS

Roughing gouge
Skew chisel, 1¼″
Spindle gouge
Straight-across and roundnose
  scrapers

6. For the most accurate fit, take the first-cup section and place the larger diameter over the lip of the second section (Illus. 286). Reduce the lip until the first section slides over it to within ⅛" of its smallest diameter.

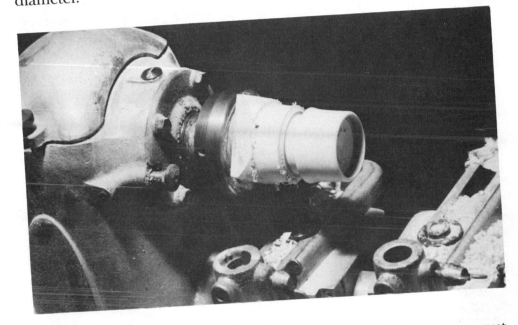

86. Size, using
ion.

7. Drill through the middle with the smaller bit and then scrape out the waste, constantly checking the wall thickness (Illus. 287). Finish by glass-papering and applying a plastic coat inside and out (see Method 4). You have now completed two sections of the cup.

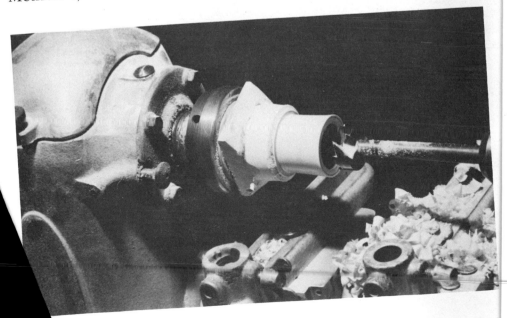

Fluted parting tool
Calipers
Sliding bevel

FINISHING

Cup: Method 4
Container: Method 1 or 4

DIFFICULTY

Grade C. To ensure that the cup will fit together perfectly, you will need to do extremely accurate work. This project is a true test of the woodturner's skill

1. Fix the blank in the lathe between centers and reduce it to the largest diameter. Square the end grain with the skew. Make the top ring of the cup first (Illus. 281); then size the next two rings from it. With the fluted parting tool, cut a groove ⅛" deep, 1¼" from the right-hand end of the cylinder. Form a very slight rim on the right-hand end, tapering the cylinder to the left. Only a gentle taper is required to form the lines of the completed cup. Turn a further slight lip at the grooved end. Glass-paper at this stage.

Illus. 281. The first ring.

2. With the 1"-saw-toothed bit, drill through the middle to a depth of 1¼" in preparation for scraping the inside. Remove the internal

OK

waste carefully to produce a thin-walled section (Illus. 282); then glass-paper and plastic-coat both the inside and outside according to Method 4 on page 214 or another method you may prefer. The cylinder may shrink as the waste is removed or if excessive heat is built up by glass-papering, so you should proceed carefully.

Illus. 282. Remove waste with bit.

3. Check the angle of the taper with a sliding bevel so that you can repeat it on the rings that follow (Illus. 283). Part off with the fluted parting tool, carefully placing your fingers around the work so that you can catch the finished piece.

Illus. 283. Measure taper angle with sliding bevel.

4. After parting the first-cup section, square the end grain with the skew and measure the smallest diameter of the first-cup section with calipers. Add ⅛" and then transfer this measurement to the end grain as a guide (Illus. 284).

Illus. 2 first sect

5. Measure 1¼" from the right-hand side and then scribe a line Reduce the cylinder to the diameter plus ⅛", which you have alrea marked on the end grain. Measure 1¼" from the right-hand and then scribe a line ⅛" deep to set the depth of the taper. (taper, at the same time forming a lip at the right-hand er previously did (Illus. 285). Check the angle of the taper sliding bevel.

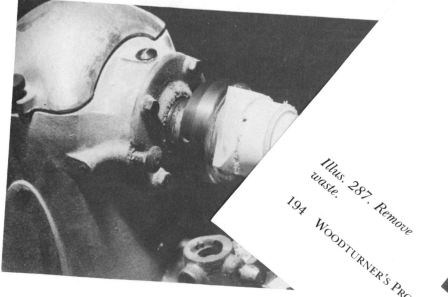

Illus. 287. Remove waste.

8. The third-cup section requires a spigot at the base, but is otherwise made in exactly the same way as the preceding two sections (Illus. 288).

Square the remaining end grain with the skew, measure the smallest internal diameter of the second section with calipers, and transfer this measurement plus ⅛″ onto the end grain. Measure 1″ from the right-hand end of the cylinder and reduce the workpiece to this diameter. Mark another line at 1″, scribe to a depth of ⅛″, and cut the taper to this depth.

Remember to form the lip the same way as you previously did. Reverse the second section onto the cylinder as you did before, reducing the lip until it reaches to within ⅛″ of the smaller diameter (refer back to Illus. 286).

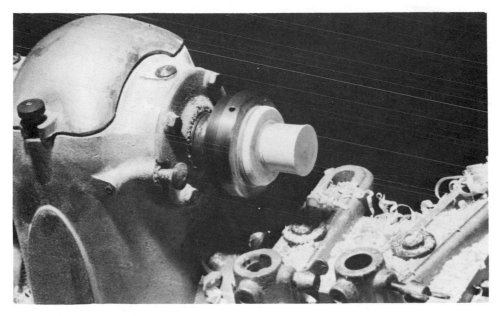

Illus. 288. Third section.

9. Drill through to a depth of ⅝″, and use a roundnose scraper to round the inside of the base (Illus. 289). Glass-paper inside and out to a finish and then form the spigot, which is 1″ long and ⅛″ deep. Undercut the base of the cup slightly to ensure a good fit into the retaining cup base, which you will make next. Plastic-coat according to Method 4 and part off.

10. Now it's time to set the cup aside and make the outer box. The blank for the box should be ⅞″ larger than the largest diameter of

the cup so that it can fully enclose the folded cup. Rough down the blank and place it into the spigot chuck to make the lid first. Drill through the middle of the workpiece and then hollow it out with a spindle gouge to a depth of 1¼″ (Illus. 290). Glass-paper and then finish completely according to Method 1 on page 213, Method 4 on page 214, or another method of your choice.

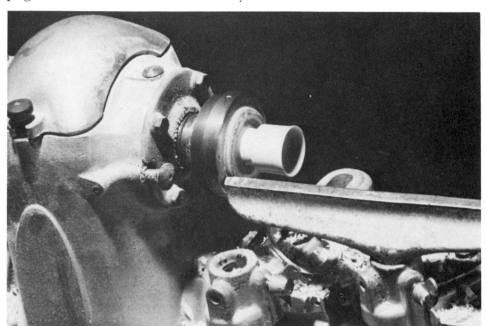

Illus. 289. Completed third section.

Illus. 290. Hollow out lid.

11. Measure 1¾″ from the right-hand end of the cylinder, scribe, and part. Square the end grain with the skew and form a rabbet to accept the lid (Illus. 291).

Illus. 291. Lid interior.

12. Drill through the middle of the workpiece and then hollow it out with the gouge to a depth that allows the top ring to be completely contained by the lid and base combined (Illus. 292). The top ring of the cup will contain the two other pieces inside its circumference. Continually remove the waste and then insert the top of the cup, enclosing it with the lid until you reach this point. Finish the interior completely and then drill through the middle to accept the spigot on the base section of the cup.

Illus. 292. Size third cup section.

13. Scribe the cylinder with a mark equal to the measurement from the lip to the base of the hole plus ³⁄₁₆″; then shape the outside of the base (Illus. 293).

Illus. 293. Shape the base.

14. Push-fit the lid and, using the tailstock spindle for support, remove the bulk of the waste (Illus. 294). Finish with the spindle gouge.

Illus. 294. Reposition the lid.

15. Glass-paper, finish, and part off the box (Illus. 295). (Methods 1 and 4 are recommended.)

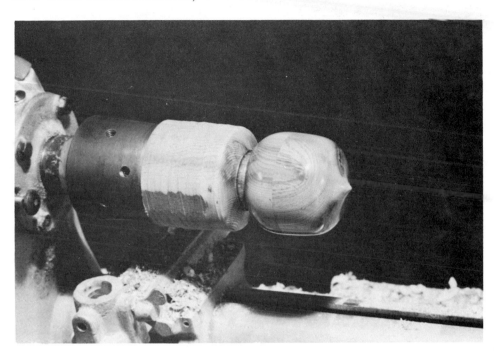

Illus. 295. Finish and part off.

16. The five components are ready for assembly (Illus. 296). The cup rings simply slide inside each other, and the bottom ring is glued into the box base after assembly.

Illus. 296. The five components.

17. Illus. 297 shows the cross section and the method of assembly.

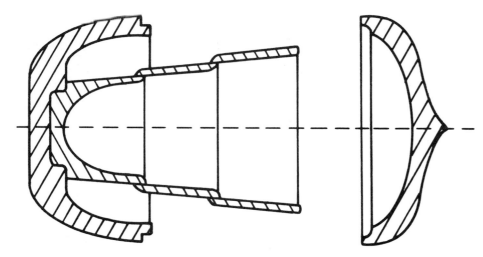

Illus. 297. Cross section.

18. The pieces rattle nicely inside the box when the lid is replaced (Illus. 298).

Illus. 298. Plan view.

43
MAGICIAN'S
EGGCUP

Illus. 299.

WOOD

Sycamore or any plain lumber
    for ebonizing
$3'' \times 3'' \times 12''$
Two plastic eggs (not wooden
    eggs because they have to be
    identical) or two table-tennis
    balls, one to be cut in half

LATHE ACCESSORIES	Split collet chuck or spigot chuck
	Revolving center
	Jacob's chuck
	Saw-toothed machine center bit
OTHER TOOLS	Roughing gouge
	Skew chisel, 1¼″
	Spindle gouge
	Beading and parting tool
	Fluted parting tool
	Domed and straight-across scraper
FINISHING	Method 4
DIFFICULTY	Very difficult. You must turn the central ring exactly so that it will fit between the lid and cup without detection.

1. Prepare the blank for the collet chuck between centers, rough it down to the largest diameter, and insert it into the chuck (Illus. 300). You should make the piece in this order: lid, central ring, and goblet base.

Illus. 300. The blank in the collet chuck.

2. To make the lid, which will accommodate half the false egg, first square the end grain with the skew, using the revolving center for

stability. Measure the largest diameter of the egg (do not cut the egg yet) and remove waste with the scraper from the end of the cylinder so that the pointed end of the egg is concealed (Illus. 301).

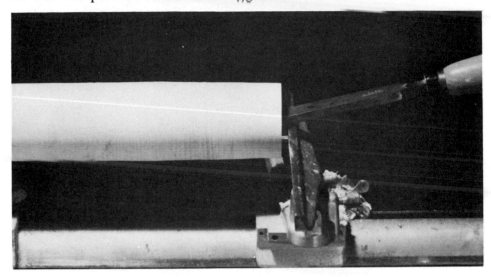

Illus. 301. Remove waste with scraper for false egg.

3. Continually offer the egg to the hole, checking for a good fit (Illus. 302). In this example, the hole that is required is 1½″ deep and 1¾″ in diameter. When you are satisfied that the egg will fit correctly, you can cut it in half with a sharp knife. You should keep the pointed end.

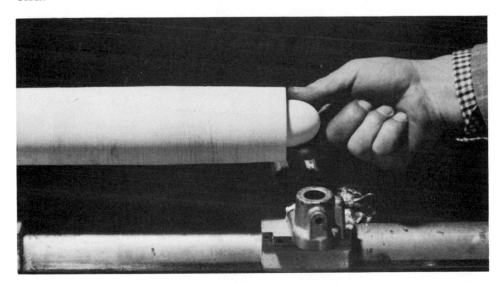

Illus. 302. Constantly check for an accurate fit.

4. Refer to Illus. 304. The end of the cylinder will form the base of the lid, which fits into the central ring. Turn a lip at the end of the cylinder ⅛″ wide to a diameter of 2¹⁄₁₆″. Measure 2¾″ from the lip and then scribe the cylinder. This line delineates the top of the lid,

including the waste that is used later when the piece is rechucked. Remove some of the waste from the lid, leaving enough for rechucking, as shown in Illus. 303. Part off and put aside.

Illus. 303. The lid roughed out.

5. The end of the cylinder should resemble the one in Illus. 304.

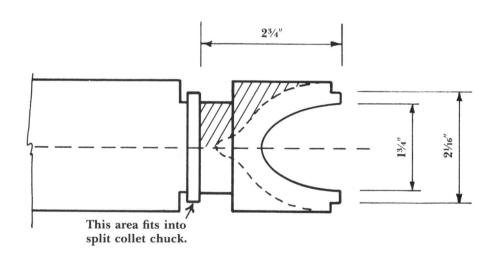

2¾"

1¾"

2¹⁄₁₆"

This area fits into
split collet chuck.

Illus. 304. Shape of lid and waste.

6. Refer to Illus. 305. You need to make the central ring next. The lid lip should fit inside the central ring. Square the end grain with the skew, and mark the outer diameter of the lid rim on the end of the cylinder. Remove the waste with the scraper to the diameter and depth of the lid rim.

Constantly offer the lid to the recess, checking for an exact fit. When you reach this point, mark the largest diameter minus ¹⁄₁₀" of the half egg's diameter on the floor of the recess. Scrape out the waste to a depth of $\frac{1}{10}''$, and enlarge the hole so that the half-egg fits into the rabbet. Drill through the middle of the rabbet to a depth of $1''$, using a $1\frac{1}{4}''$-saw-toothed machine center bit (Illus. 306).

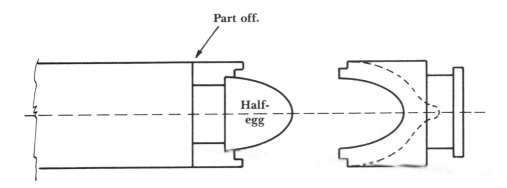

Illus. 305. Egg not glued in at this stage.

Illus. 306. Drill through middle of rabbet.

7. Mark the outside of the central ring with two lines (Illus. 307). The first line equals the depth from the end of the cylinder to the bottom of the half-egg rabbet; the second line is equal to the depth of the lid rim. Part off at the second mark, as shown in Illus. 305.

8. Note the two rabbets and the hollow middle of the ring in Illus. 305.

9. Rechuck the lid and push-fit the ring into its base (Illus. 308). True the outside of the cylinder and square the end grain of the ring with the skew.

10. Refer to Illus. 309. Mark the outside diameter of the lid lip on the end grain of the ring; in this example, it's $2\frac{1}{16}''$. Measure the second

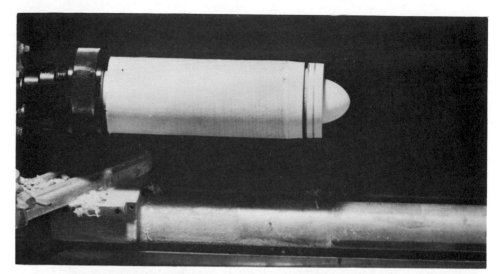

Illus. 307. Ring marked and ready for parting.

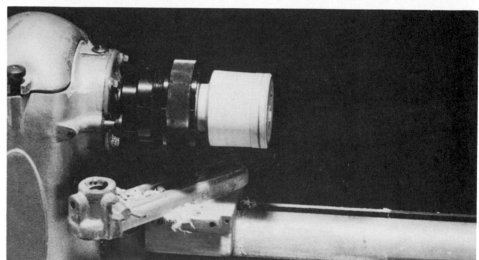

Illus. 308. Rechuck the lid and push-fit the ring.

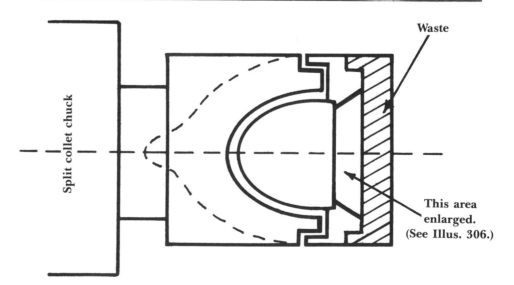

Split collet chuck

Waste

This area enlarged. (See Illus. 306.)

Illus. 309. False egg recess.

egg and also mark the diameter on the ring. Enlarge the hollow middle of the ring to accept the second egg as far as its halfway point (Illus. 310). The hole will require a taper, which will follow the shape of the second egg. Be very careful not to cut away the small rabbet, upon which the half-egg stands. Scribe and mark the cylinder ⅛″ from the end; then form a lip to the exact diameter of the previously made lip, which is 2¹⁄₁₆″. Remove the workpiece from the chuck.

Illus. 310. Trial-fit the second egg into ring.

11. In Illus. 309, note the taper inside the ring and the false egg resting on its rabbet.

12. Rechuck the remaining base section, square the end grain with the skew, and proceed as you would for a standard goblet. Form a recess in the end grain to accept the central ring lip and then enlarge the central hole to accept the second egg. Frequently check the egg in the hole because the hole must be deep enough to allow insertion to its midpoint. Check to make sure that the egg will fit into the ring, allowing the ring to meet the goblet rim exactly flush (Illus. 311).

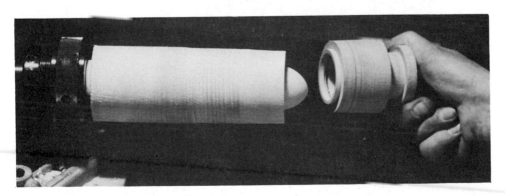

Illus. 311. Trial-fit the second egg into goblet.

13. Refer to Illus. 312. Remove the egg and push-fit the lid and ring, bringing up the revolving center for stability. Mark the base, the stem, and the depth of the cup on the outside of the cylinder (Illus. 313); then transfer these marks to the tool rest for reference.

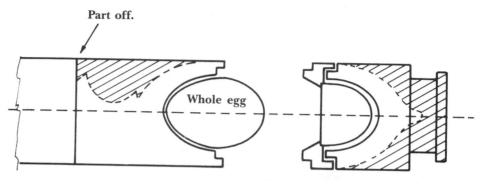

Part off.

Whole egg

Illus. 312. Egg-cup profile.

Illus. 313. Assemble the components for final turning.

14. Delineate the final outside shape (Illus. 312).

15. The finished outside shape is shown in Illus. 314.

Illus. 314. Final shape—note holding pip.

16. Form the camouflage beads (Illus. 315), finish with abrasives, and ebonize according to Method 4 or another method you may prefer. Part off and assemble, gluing the half-egg into its recess with epoxy cement.

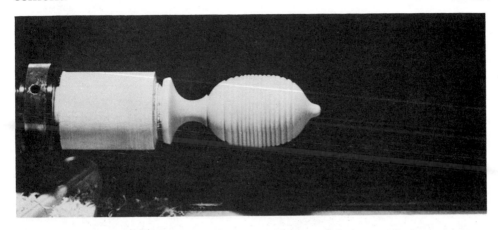

Illus. 315. The camouflage beads.

17. See the three components of the eggcup in Illus. 316.

Illus. 316. The three components.

The trick: Hold the goblet in one hand and both the lid and ring in the other. Show the audience the egg in the goblet, and invite someone to remove the egg. Replace the lid on the goblet and slide the fingers of your hand holding the goblet up to grasp the ring. Say the magic words or wave your wand and then remove the lid to reveal another (half) egg. The beads on the outside of the piece confuse the eye—with a little practice, this can be a very impressive trick.

44
PLUGS

When a workpiece has a large hole drilled through the middle, you need to use a plug to fill the hole so that the workpiece can be reversed between centers. Any scrap of moderately hard lumber is suitable for making a plug, so it's a good idea to keep a variety of sizes in your tool box. To make a plug, follow these instructions.

1. Rough down a piece of square stock to a cylinder (Illus. 317) and then delineate the middle with a parting tool.

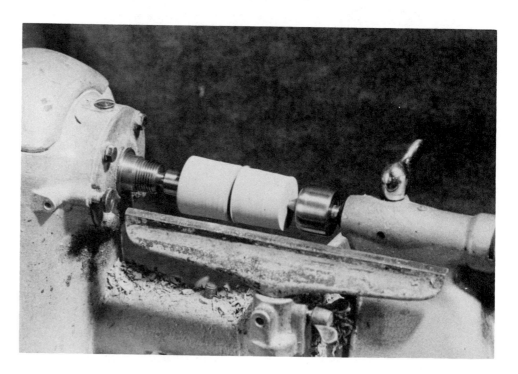

Illus. 317. Rough down to a cylinder.

2. Taper the right-hand section from right to left (Illus. 318).

Illus. 318. Taper right-hand section.

3. Taper the left-hand section from left to right (Illus. 319), and then part off.

The finish from the roughing gouge is adequate and will provide a suitable grip. Note that one section will have a key for the driving center and that the other will have a key for the revolving center.

Illus. 319. Taper left-hand section.

45
FINISHING

MATERIALS
Use open-coat garnet or aluminum-oxide paper in 100-to-320-grit sizes. You can also use glass paper instead of garnet paper.

Finishes
Cellulose sanding sealer is cellulose based (amyl acetate) with an inert filler.

Friction polish is similar to a French polish, but does not have the dragging problems associated with French polishes. There are various brand names.

Wax blocks are made with one-part carnauba wax and three-parts beeswax; then the substance is covered with wood turpentine, heated in a double boiler, and poured into a mould.

Two-part plastic finish (**black or clear**) is a superior finish, which is moisture-, chemical-, and heat-resistant. Follow maker's instructions.

Danish oil is similar to boiled linseed oil, but has dryers added to give a quick, high shine, which is water-repellent. Ideal for salad bowls.

Polyurethane varnish (**matt or gloss**) can be an acceptable finish on light, blind, or curtain pulls and other small items. French polish sealer (shellac) can be used instead of cellulose sanding sealer, but it's not as effective. It can also be used underneath polyurethane varnish.

Steel wool (**000**) can be used to create a scratch-free surface after using sealers.

METHODS

Method 1

This is the most frequently used finishing method for objects that are handled often or should not get damp. It can be rejuvenated by a good-quality cream furniture polish.

		LATHE	
		Turning	Stopped
a)	Finish with 320-grit finishing paper.	X	
b)	Coat liberally with cellulose sanding sealer. Apply with brush or absorbent cotton.		X
c)	Apply wood shavings from lathe to dry and burnish.	X	
d)	Apply 000 steel wool to flatten the surface.	X	
e)	Dust down with clean cloth.	X	
f)	Apply friction polish sparingly with absorbent cotton.		X
g)	Apply pressure with same absorbent cotton until a high shine is reached.	X	
h)	Apply wax blocks.	X	
i)	Polish with soft cloth for high shine.	X	

Method 2

This is an oil finish for salad or fruit bowls, which can be rejuvenated with cooking, olive, or linseed oil. Follow steps a–e in Method 1, and then proceed with this method.

		LATHE	
		Turning	Stopped
f)	Apply oil sparingly with absorbent cotton.		X
g)	Apply pressure with same absorbent cotton.	X	
h)	Polish with soft cloth.	X	

This finish will improve if you leave the piece for 24 hours and then sparingly apply a second coat, on or off the lathe, and then polish it with a soft cloth.

Method 3

Polyurethane varnish is a hard-wearing finish, which you can use instead of Method 4, but not for goblets.

		LATHE	
		Turning	**Stopped**
a)	Finish with 320-grit finishing paper.	X	
b)	Apply French polish sanding sealer with brush or absorbent cotton.		X
c)	Buff with cotton cloth.	X	

Remove the piece from the lathe and give it at least two coats.

Method 4

Two-part plastic (black for ebonizing, or clear) is an ideal finish for goblets and articles likely to be handled with wet or damp hands.

		LATHE	
		Turning	**Stopped**
a)	Finish with 320-grit garnet paper.	X	
b)	Apply mixed plastic with soft brush, turning lathe by hand.		
c)	Remove and allow to harden.		
d)	Give a second coat according to maker's instructions.		X
e)	Remount on lathe and buff, using compound supplied by makers. Care is required because you could cut back to bare wood.	X	
f)	Using polymer liquid car polish, buff to a high shine.	X	

Friction Polishing

One of the most popular finishes for turned work involves the application of sanding sealer, friction polish, and wax. This is a reasonably durable finish for items that will not be excessively handled or immersed in washing solvents, and can be rejuvenated by the application of a good furniture wax polish. You should not use silicone sprays or other synthetic polishes.

The following sequence of photos shows the method of application. Before applying abrasives or polishes, always remove the hand-rest.

1. Finish the workpiece with the tools as far as possible; then use open-coat garnet paper or glass paper for a fine finish. For safety reasons, be sure to remove the tool rest while applying finishes. The lathe should be revolving at a high-speed setting (Illus. 320). To remove any rings left by the abrasive paper, stop the lathe and glass-paper along the direction of the grain.

Illus. 320. Open-coat garnet paper—lathe turning.

2. Dust the surface of the work and then apply sanding sealer with a brush or absorbent cotton. The lathe should not be turning (Illus. 321).

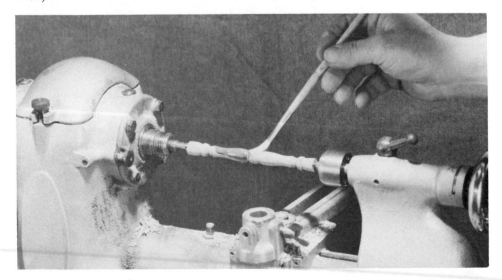

Illus. 321. Sanding sealer—lathe stopped.

3. Start the lathe and then pick up a handful of shavings and burnish to a shine (Illus. 322). Be careful not to generate too much heat, although some heat is desirable to dry the sanding sealer. The lathe should be turning.

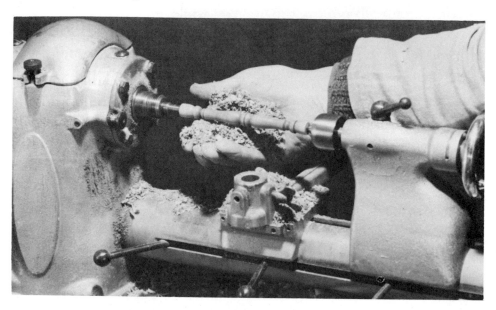

*Illus. 322. Burnish-
ing—lathe turning.*

4. Remove small pieces of shavings with an old toothbrush and then clean out the crevices, with the lathe turning (Illus. 323).

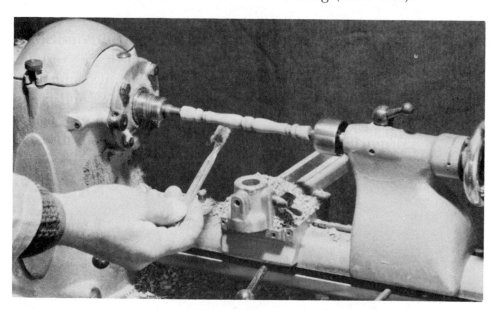

*Illus. 323. Cleaning—
lathe turning.*

5. Matt down the surface with steel wool, with the lathe turning (Illus. 324). Now, stop the lathe and finish by rubbing along the direction of the grain.

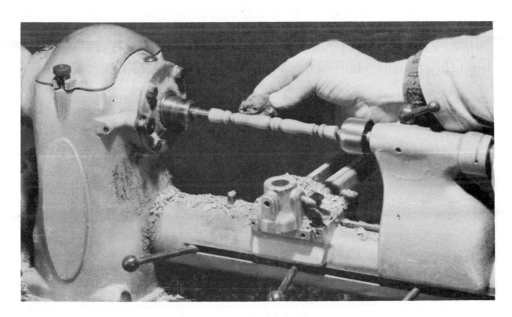

6. Shake up the bottle of friction polish and lightly moisten a piece of absorbent cotton with some of the liquid. With the lathe stopped (to avoid a shower of polish), sparingly apply the polish; then quickly switch on the lathe and buff to a high shine with the same absorbent cotton (Illus. 325).

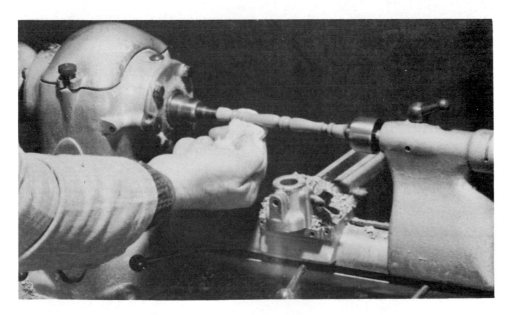

Illus. 325. Stop lathe to apply polish—lathe turning to buff shine.

7. You can buy the wax or make it yourself using a mixture of ¼ part carnauba wax and ¾ part beeswax that is covered with genuine turpentine and heated in a double boiler.

With the lathe still turning, apply the wax block evenly over the surface of the work, removing excess wax with a cloth (Illus. 326).

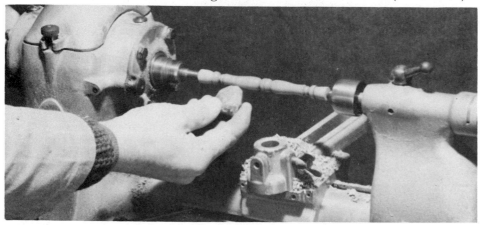

Illus. 326. Wax block— lathe turning.

8. Clean out the crevices with a flat stick where wax has accumulated. The lathe should be turning (Illus. 327).

Illus. 327. Cleaning crevices—lathe turning.

9. With the lathe still turning, polish the wax to a high shine with a clean cloth (Illus. 328).

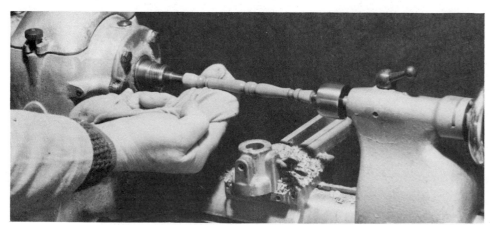

Illus. 328. Polishing wax coat—lathe turning.

METRIC EQUIVALENCY CHART

mm—millimetres   **cm—centimetres**

INCHES TO MILLIMETRES AND CENTIMETRES

inches	mm	cm	inches	cm	inches	cm
⅛	3	0.3	9	22.9	30	76.2
¼	6	0.6	10	25.4	31	78.7
⅜	10	1.0	11	27.9	32	81.3
½	13	1.3	12	30.5	33	83.8
⅝	16	1.6	13	33.0	34	86.4
¾	19	1.9	14	35.6	35	88.9
⅞	22	2.2	15	38.1	36	91.4
1	25	2.5	16	40.6	37	94.0
1¼	32	3.2	17	43.2	38	96.5
1½	38	3.8	18	45.7	39	99.1
1¾	44	4.4	19	48.3	40	101.6
2	51	5.1	20	50.8	41	104.1
2½	64	6.4	21	53.3	42	106.7
3	76	7.6	22	55.9	43	109.2
3½	89	8.9	23	58.4	44	111.8
4	102	10.2	24	61.0	45	114.3
4½	114	11.4	25	63.5	46	116.8
5	127	12.7	26	66.0	47	119.4
6	152	15.2	27	68.6	48	121.9
7	178	17.8	28	71.1	49	124.5
8	203	20.3	29	73.7	50	127.0

ABOUT THE AUTHORS

Phil Jones was born in South Wales, and comes from a family of building-industry craftsmen. After serving a 5-year apprenticeship as a carpenter and joiner and then working in the trade for 12 years, he entered Shoreditch College, located near Windsor, England, where he studied to be a crafts teacher. He obtained a distinction in advanced crafts from the college, and has been teaching in schools in

Illus. 329. Phil Jones.

the county of Hertfordshire for 15 years. He also has a B.A. degree in education and technology from the Open University.

As a tutor in wood turning for the Hertfordshire Education Authority, he has given intensive 2- and 3-day wood-turning courses for crafts, design, and technology teachers. In addition, he sells his own work at crafts fairs and exhibitions in England and demonstrates lathe work to large audiences at specialist woodworking shows.

Charles Mercer was born in London, England. He has worked with the Hertfordshire County Forestry Department and at a busy lumber-importing agency in London. He now operates his own business as a free-lance consultant, specializing in the lumber trade and the supply of wood-turning and wood-carving tools.

After attending a wood-turning course with Phil Jones, he approached Mr. Jones with the idea for this book. Charles Mercer regularly contributes articles to several trade magazines. He took the photographs and prepared the text for this book.

Illus. 330. Charles Mercer.

INDEX